★ *The* ★

BOSOX CLUB

=== **50 YEARS** ===

The BoSox Club — 50 Years
By Bill Nowlin

ISBN 978-1-57940-253-2
Ebook 978-1-57940-254-9

Cover and book design: Gilly Rosenthol

Front cover photographs:
Dom DiMaggio and Johnny Pesky at Fenway Park, 2002. Photograph by
Tim Samway.
Rick Porcello at BoSox Club event, Summer 2016, with 2017-18 club president
Mike Vining. Photograph by Cindy Loo, courtesy of Boston Red Sox.

Back cover photograph: Carol J. Merletti

Photography credits:

Boston Red Sox: Dedication page, 59, 66, 68, 70, 99, 100, 101, 102, 103,
104, 105, 106.
Bruce Donahue: 98 (top), 107.
Gordon McKay: 57.
Jim Prime: 56.
Tim Samway: 80, 81, 89, 90, 91, 92, 93, 94, 95.
United States Postal Service – 98 (bottom).
Angels Booster Club – 114.
Paul Gardner – 148.
Mona Neill – 154.
Toronto Blue Jays – 156.
Alicia Vining – 97.

ROUNDER

Rounder Books
29 Lancaster Street
Cambridge MA 02140

★ *The* ★

BOSOX CLUB

50 YEARS

BY BILL NOWLIN

Table of Contents

The BoSox Club - 50 Years
By Bill Nowlin

The BoSox Club's beginnings..1

The Earliest Fan Clubs in Boston..6

The Royal Rooters 16

The Winter League 31

John S. Dooley.. 33

The Bull Pen A.C..41

"The Bleacherites".. 42

The Lido Beachcombers A.C... 43

The Red Sox One Half Century Club..44

The Boston Braves 45

The BoSox Club - First Look 47

The BLOHARDS...49

Bluenose Bosox Brotherhood 55

The BoSox Club 57

The First Spring Training Trip and the Second Season................ 62

Closing Out the 1960s and Into the 1970s.. 65

The 1980s...73

1990 and the 90s.. 78

The Year 2000 and Beyond.. 82

Into the Second Decade of the 21st Century.................................... 96

BoSox Club Man of the Year 108

BoSox Club Presidents 110

The Jernegan Award 111

A Summary Look at Fan and Booster Clubs Around
Major-League Baseball...113

Notes 162

This book is dedicated to the memory of "Bresh" — Richard L. Bresciani (January 16, 1938 — November 29, 2014), longtime liaison between the Red Sox and the BoSox Club, a vice president of the Red Sox, an inductee in the Red Sox Hall of Fame, and the BoSox Club Man of the Year in 1989.

The BoSox Club – 50 Years

By Bill Nowlin

In the year 2017, the BoSox Club website presented a capsule view of its history:

In 1966, the Red Sox had a disastrous season losing 90 games and finished next to last in the American League. Attendance had fallen drastically. The outlook for the team was bleak. In the winter of 1966-67, the Red Sox assembled a group of local businessmen and formed the BoSox Club of Boston, hoping to give a "boost" and to increase ticket sales throughout Boston and New England. The BoSox Club was first organized by Bill Crowley, the Director of Public Relations for the Red Sox, along with broadcaster Ken Coleman, former Red Sox Dom DiMaggio and Ted Lepcio, and Tom Feenan Sr., Harry Carlson, Bob Cheyne, Brad Jernegan and a few others. In 1967, the first year, the club signed on 305 enthusiastic members from all around New England. Officers were elected including Dom DiMaggio, President; Bradford C. Jernegan, Vice President; Larry Polans, Vice President; and Truman Casner, Legal Advisor. Directors of the club included Bernard Baldwin, Dean M. Boylan, Thomas J. Feenan, Robert Cheyne, Clarence March, and James Kelso.[1]

We all know what happened during the 1967 season. The Impossible Dream team took the region by storm winning 90 games and the American League pennant. The BoSox Club doesn't take credit for this incredible season, but we do think it is a curious coincidence!

Since those early days, the BoSox Club has continued to carry out its mission and grow in membership. Today we are recognized by the Red Sox as the Official Booster Club of the Team and we contribute to a variety of charitable causes through many events and special programs. Mostly though, the BoSox Club continues to provide the most intimate "behind the ropes" experience for our members through our monthly luncheons, spring training trips, BBQs and more.

The BoSox Club's Beginnings

As long as there have been baseball clubs—amateur or professional—there have been groups of fans (they were called "cranks" in the early days) to support them. The same is true, of course, for teams or clubs in other sports. At times, that support is genteel. At other times, it can get rowdy—or even lead to battle as it did in the "soccer war" of 1969 when armed conflict broke out between Honduras and El Salvador, whose airplanes actually dropped bombs on the Honduran capital, Tegucigalpa.

In 2017, Boston Red Sox fans celebrate 50 years of the venerable BoSox Club, founded in 1967. It's one of the longest-lived "booster clubs" in baseball circles, though the club readily acknowledges its roots in Red Sox rooting and also a direct debt due its immediate predecessor, Cleveland's Wahoo Club founded in 1962.

Red Sox broadcaster Ken Coleman was a native of Quincy, Massachusetts (born 1925), but had worked broadcasting Cleveland Browns games for 14 years, from 1952 through 1965. In March 1966, he was hired to become the voice of the Boston Red Sox.

The 1966 season saw the Red Sox finish in ninth place (lower on the ladder than many fans today can remember, spared only a last-place (10th place) finish by virtue of finishing a half-game ahead of the even-more-lowly New York Yankees. The Sox were 72-90 on the season.

Jose Santiago (12-13) led the team in wins. Jim Lonborg (10-10) ranked second. No one else even won nine. Tony Conigliaro led the team in home runs (28) and RBIs (93). George Scott wasn't far behind—27 and 90. Yaz had 16 homers and drove in 80. No one hit .300 and the team as a whole batted .240. After 146 games, the Sox had even dumped their manager, Billy Herman.

Meanwhile, the team's Triple-A team—the Toronto Maple Leafs—had put together an excellent season, under manager Dick Williams. They were a relatively young team, who finished one game out of first place, but won the International League finals.

Williams was hired to manage the 1967 Red Sox. And in February, a new Red Sox booster club was announced.

In December 2001, Ken told the story of how it began:

> I was a member of the Wahoo Club in Cleveland. It was an Indians booster club and when I came to Boston, I spoke with Bill Crowley, who was the public relations director of the Red Sox and told him about the Wahoo Club and what they were doing. In 1966, the Red Sox weren't doing well at all. So we got a group of people together up in the old press room at Fenway and we put in a call to [Cleveland GM] Gabe Paul and [former major league and Cleveland business executive] Al Rosen on a speaker phone, and they spoke to us and we started the club. They told us what the Wahoo Club was and what it was for.
>
> They didn't have many members. Sometimes we'd only have 10 or 12. It was not a big club. Cleveland is not Boston, in terms of things like that. We never got as many as 50 people, not that I recall. They were trying to get it going. I used to play a lot of racquetball and I'd go down to the Y, and guys would say to me, "Oh, I guess the team's at home, huh?" Back in those days in Cleveland, in that stadium, one of the things that made it a very difficult situation for them was the fact that people would go to the games and if there were 10,000 people at the game—which was rare that there would be that many—there'd be 70,000 empty seats. Crowds draw crowds. When you go down there and there's nobody there...the crowds were sparse most of the time.
>
> We held the Club meetings at a hotel downtown, and I think it appealed mostly to people who worked downtown. They had lunch every month or two. I'm not even sure if it's still in existence.

The Bosox Club has been the most successful club in the country. When we started the club, we met at first at the Somerset Hotel.

Dominic DiMaggio was the president and we had a board of governors. Bob Cheyne was one of them; he was an executive at the old WHDH. Brad Jernigan was in the banking business. They were always lunch meetings. The first year that we had them on a regular basis, Dick Williams never missed a meeting. He was at every one of them. I don't recall how many people came to those early meetings; there were always a lot of people.

They send kids to Mike Andrews Baseball Camp. The by-laws of the club is to help baseball on all levels. They have a thing for the winners of the Boston Park League, different leagues.

In Winter Haven, the Bosox Club used to take a group of people—they paid for it—that went down there for a week and went to games and they'd have a banquet down there in the evening. Dick Bresciani could fill you in on that stuff.[2]

Indeed, the Wahoo Club is still in existence, and several other major-league ballclubs have similar organizations. We will turn to a look around baseball, after more fully exploring the history of fan organizations in the Boston area.

The Earliest Fan Clubs in Boston

It does appear that the Royal Rooters were one of the first organized fan clubs in Boston. There certainly were "fans" of note before the Royal Rooters were formed. In September 1889, the *Boston Herald* devoted considerable space to "Some Patrons of the Game" in its September 12 issue.

These fans are portrayed as individuals, and had not yet grouped into friends of the game who might meet together, either at the ballpark or outside of confines of the South End Grounds.

SOME PATRONS OF THE GAME.

People Who Like to Sit in the Sound End Grand Stand.

The Well Known Followers of the Boston Club and Their Individual Characteristics

Base ball is one of the most fascinating of pastimes, and its devotees in this city can be reckoned by the thousands. There is no city in the country that can boast of so many regular attendants. The game is deservedly popular, for few cities have such excellent surroundings for the game as has Boston. The location of the grounds is near the residential district, and most of the patrons can go home to their supper with but little delay. The grand pavilion is the most costly in the country; its erection was a great improvement, and did a great deal to attract a fine class of patrons to the grounds. The nine has been strengthened season after season, and thereby the interest in the sport has not only been sustained, but increased.

There are many among the patrons who are constant attendants, who can be seen in the same places day after day as surely as there is to be a game. A visit to any contest will reveal this. Among the more conspicuous of the regular attendants of the game is Mr. Arthur Dixwell. Outside of the players on the contesting nines, there is no one who is asked for as often as Mr. Dixwell. "Where is he?" and "Who is he?" are two questions that are constantly asked. Mr. Dixwell occupies a seat in the section adjoining that of the reporters, where he can hear everything that is going on among the reporters, and at the same time receive the information by wire as to the progress of the game in other cities. He is a gentleman of means and passionately fond of the national game. He said at the commencement of the season that if the Bostons would put a nine of championship caliber into the field, he would abandon a projected trip to Europe and accompany the club on its travels. This he has done, and he has enjoyed himself immensely. He has given his favorites more encouragement this year, in the games away from home, than they ever got before, and his cry of "Hi, Hi." has become known throughout the land. Fancy a robust gentleman of medium height, wearing a light beard, rising to his feet with every good play of his favorites and vigorously applauding, and, at the same time, indulging in a vocal accompaniment. He does not "let himself out" in this city when on the road, for there is not the necessity of encouragement in the game in this city as there is abroad.

He Knows All of the Players,

and frequently bestows upon them boxes of the choicest cigars as a form of approval of their work. Not long ago he presented to each of the Boston players a fine bat bag. He is a base ball statistician, and at home or abroad he is surrounded by numerous record books, from which he can compile at a moment's notice the individual record of every league player to date.

Sitting just behind the Boston directors is an elderly gentleman, with hair and mustache plentifully streaked with white. He has a genial eye and a very pleasant address. The gentleman is Mr. George B. [could be H.] Lloyd, the "Ferguson" whose letters in the HERALD have delighted so many thousand readers. Many people thought that it was the umpire, "Bob" Ferguson, who wrote the letters in question, and many were amazed that the old ball tosser was capable of such excellent work. Mr. Lloyd has for many years been a warm admirer of the game. It is very rarely that he misses a contest. In the days when it was nip and tuck between the Bostons and the Providences, no Bostonian made so many pilgrimages to Providence as Mr. Lloyd. He does not give vent to his feelings in a game as does his friend Dixwell. He assumes an attitude of the deepest interest, and his only manner of showing his feelings is by the play of his features. Once in a while he will venture some bright remark to President Soden, who sits directly in front of him. Mr. Lloyd was once a stockholder in the Boston club. His share was afterward purchased at a generous figure, and he is now a life season ticket holder. Mr. Lloyd's family is almost as interested in the game as he is. He has two sons who are expert players, one of them having been for several years a crack first baseman. His daughter, too, knows how to keep score and discusses base ball matters very intelligently. The young lady is rarely absent from the game, and generally occupies a seat by the side of her father, perfectly fearless in the face of the hot foul balls that frequently come flying around her.

There is no noisier attendant at a ball game than George W. Floyd, the theatrical manager, who was for so many years connected with Nat Goodwin. Floyd cannot take in many games on account of his professional duties, but he makes his presence felt. He sits in the front row of the grand pavilion and keeps up a continual chatter. Again and again the question has been asked: "Why doesn't somebody shut that fellow up?" and the answer is already ready: "Why, that is only George Floyd!" Floyd is one of the jolliest and finniest fellows living, and he keeps up a running tirade at the visiting players that does not cease until the game is ended. Director Conant is

Always on Pins and Needles

when Floyd is around. Floyd cares as little for Sergt. Curry as for Conant, and always manages to send him away smiling. Floyd always "roots" for Kelly. It was Floyd who arranged the great reception and presentation that Mike got after his return from the first trip he made with the Bostons. It is said that Floyd seriously contemplated at one time starting a paper of his own, just to show reporters how base ball should be reported. No one was happier over the victory of the Bostons this week than Floyd.

Who does not know the genial George Appleton? Whenever he can find time to leave the cares of his business, George can be found in a seat in the front row of the grand pavilion at the right of the telegraphers. He is a bosom friend of President Soden, who always had a warm opinion of Appleton, and who values his judgment highly. It was Mr. Appleton who went to Washington and arranged to have the Detroit players come to this city. Mr. Appleton was once the official scorer of the famous Lowell club, the crack amateur club of Boston toward the close of the sixties. There is no more enthusiastic supporter of the Boston Base Ball Club and its fortunes.

C. J. ("Jimmy") Connelly of the Adams House is another fixture, and no game would be actually complete without his presence. He has a seat next to that of Director Conant. It is rarely that the two disagree upon a decision, and it is rarely, therefore, that an umpire is right. If anything should happen to Mr. Conant, Connelly could well fill his shoes. He has his seat for the season, and nothing but sickness or absence from town will find his seat unoccupied.

Mr. Jacob P. Bates of the frim of Cobb, Bates & Yerra has for a long time been a warm admirer and constant patron of the game, and he greatly enjoys a fine contest. He does not confine himself to one seat, or to any particular portion of the pavilion, as do most of the regular attendants, but he takes the chair assigned to him at the box office, and is happy.

Henry C. Barnabee and W. H. McDonald of the Bostonians have found their chief pleasure this summer is attending the ball games, and they have not found it too much trouble to make the trip from the Atlantic House, Nantasket Beach, daily, and, no matter how threatening the weather, they have been at their posts, and this has been at the extreme lower right-hand corner of the pavilion, just back of the Boston players.

The actors' contingent is always large. The members of the theatrical profession always enjoy a good ball game, gentlemen and ladies alike, and they can always be found in large numbers at the contests. Jack Mason likes to be on hand; Maurice Barrymore finds it base ball one of his greatest delights; Digby Bell and De Wolf Hopper are

Critics Who Cannot Be Excelled,

and Forrest Robinson has been a constant attendant at the game this summer. One of the best posted of the profession on base ball matters is George Wilson of the Boston Museum, and there isn't a point in the game that he does not carefully watch and digest. The faces of Treasurer Quincy Kilby of the Boston Theatre, Manager William Harris of the Howard Atheneum, James A. Blake of the Globe Theatre are familiar ones. Once in a while, Mr. Eugene Tompkins of the Boston Theatre will find recreation at the South End ball grounds, and so will Ms. Isaac Rich and Charles J. Rich of the Hollis Street Theatre, Harry M'Glenen of the Boston Theatre is occasionally seen at the games, but it is young Harry who is the base ball crank of the family, while Ed is not infrequently seen in the pavilion. Gas Engineer Shea of the Boston Museum knows a thing or two about the game and is an excellent scorer. Murray and Murray, "Our Irish Visitors," are great friends of Kelly and will go miles to see him play. Edgar L. Davenport, that favorite of the Boston Museum company, enjoys a good game and often attends.

Mr. John Rogers, a warm friend of Director Conant, is one of the few privileged to take a seat in the director's box whenever he visits the grounds. Mr. Rogers is one of the best posted of critics on base ball matters.

Capt. Frank Briggs is, and has for years been, a chum of George Billings, the popular clerk of the Boston Base Ball Club, and he has a seat reserved for him in the front row, next to George Appleton.

Few of the many constant patrons have been more faithful in their attendance than Mr. George H. Munroe, a veteran journalist. He is a veteran also as far as his love for the game is concerned, and he faces the foul balls from a seat in front of the wire with a courage as undaunted as the bravest, It was Mr. Munroe who, as a member of the state Senate, succeeded in pushing through that body the articles of incorporation of the Boston Base Ball Association, and he had no easy task, there being a bitter opposition. Mr. Munroe has watched the game so long that he is very familiar with all the clubs, the players and their history, and he is a scorer equal to the best. The game and the club have few friends more loyal than he.

"Jim" Russell, one of the attaches of the mechanical department of the Boston Theatre, is also an attache of the Boston Base Ball Club, for there has been no one more unwavering in his allegiance than he.

He Is Always Present at the Games,

and if a register had been made of the number of games he has attended since the club was formed, it may well be doubted if any one would have a better record.

Fritz Giese, the well known cellist, is always sure to occupy a seat in the front row, near the Boston players. He knows all of the players, and he greatly admires John Clarkson. Boston's crack pitcher receives heartier applause from Fritz than from any one else.

There is no spectator who attracts more attention than Mr. Fred W. Goodwin. With his whiskers cut in English fashion, and his tall white hat, he looks like a Vanderbilt or some other great magnate. Fred is well fixed in this world's goods, and he loves nothing better than a good game of ball. He is always sure to be on hand.

East Boston is well represented by J. B. Maccabe. He is generally in the centre of a group on the right field bleaching boards. He rarely misses a game except when he has to go West in his capacity as first vice-president of the National Editorial Association, of which he is one of the most brilliant workers.

"Cloakman's corner" has come to be a prominent feature of the grand stand. It is located just above the benches of the Boston players. The patrons of the corner are generally Billy Quigley, Emmett Driscoll, Sam Levy, George Hurll and their immediate friends. They have a standing agreement that this particular portion of the grand stand shall be reserved for them at every game. They can always be found in their seats about half an hour before the game commences, as there is nothing which so delights the heart of a "cloakman" as to witness a fine exhibition of practice play. They all receive good salaries, but very few of them keep bank accounts. They are high livers and smoke the best Havanas. Emmett Driscoll is a Boston boy, short of stature, slim in build, and always dresses in the latest fashion. Emmett has not a musical voice, but it has a certain amount of charming persuasiveness about it which charms all his customers. Billy Quigley is of medium height, fair complexion, and a coal black mustache lies in calm repose just under a finely shaped nose. Billy does not say much when the boys are at play, but he has a keen appreciation of excellent work just the same. His head is full of statistics. "Stony" Hurll is a very successful salesman. The sum of his yearly earnings would be given if the writer was assured it would not create a feeling of jealousy. "Stony's" head is a mass of light brown curls, and he has a small mustache of the same hue. He is a great lover of base ball and takes no chances of missing a play by getting in late. If "Stony" says a thing is so, it goes for a fact without further dispute. He is a born base ball crank, and at one time did a little ball tossing on his own account. He understands all the fine points of the play and is

An Authority Among the "Cloaksmen"

whenever a dispute comes up. Sam Levy is "dead gone" on the game, and there are very few contests on the South end grounds which Sam does not see. This, of course, is in confidence, as his house thinks he is hunting customers so long as the species are to be found about. Sam pays a good deal of attention to his dress. There are no chestnuts about his personal adornments. He is a good hearted fellow, and a great favorite among the guild. He shouts for the Boston nine.

Mr. Herbert C. Leeds, one of the finest athletes who ever entered Harvard College, and a shortstop of such a kind as has not been seen in that institution since he left it, is one of the most discriminating patrons of the game, and when he is in the city there is nothing that has superior attractions for him. It was he who first suggested the advisability of doing away with the foul tip as tending to help the batting, in fact, he advocated what Mr. A. G. Spalding is now doing, the advisability of doing away with all kinds of foul balls. His first suggestion was adopted, and it remains to be seen if it will be followed as a whole. Mr. Leeds always sits directly behind the Boston players, and there is seated next to him, generally, Mr. Robert C. Hooper, a constant attendant at the matches and another Harvard man.

Of the city fathers there is no one in the upper branch so fond of the game as Alderman McLaughlin. He wants to see our boys win, and he was in New York in the last series to cheer them on to victory.

Many find the upper tier of the pavilion the best position from which to see the game. The view does possess many advantages over what can be seen from the lower deck. Here can be found very often Benjamin Radford, Paul's father, Percy Thayer and Tommy Huggins.

The attendance of ladies has never been so large as at this season. The most constant of attendants have been, as might be expected, the wives of the players. Mrs. Ganzel and Mrs. Bennett generally sit together. Mrs. M. J. Kelly occupies a seat to the right wing, while Mrs. Richardson finds it more convenient to sit behind the wire, as does also Mrs. Radbourn. Mrs. Clarkson is generally accompanied by a sister or one or more of her friends, very often by Mrs. John F. Morrill, the two being very close friends. There are two ladies in the right wing who have witnessed almost every game the Bostons have played this season, and whom the writer saw at Staten Island. Mrs. B. Leighton Beal, the wife of a well known journalist, keeps a score in a manner than a book-keeper might well envy, so neat and accurate is her method. Miss Bella Morse is

Another Accomplished Scorer,

well qualified to write up a game, in case a regular newspaper scorer wants a day off. Mrs. George W. Floyd does not sit by the side of her better half when she witnesses a game. She could not stand it very long, he makes so much noise. She gets a place by herself, with Mrs. Kelly generally as her companion. She is an expert scorer.

Among other familiar faces in almost daily attendance there may be mentioned: Councilmen Desmond and Sprague, Harry Cohen, Tony Marsh, Jack Keeler, Col. Charles H. Taylor, Steve Sherman, Robert Weiner, F. P. Ewing, John F. Dever, Charles N. Perkins, James Coane, Albert E. Pennell, J. B. Archibald, Thomas G. Clarkson (father of "our" John), Julian B. Harr, J. C. Haynes, Louis Hecht, Jr., E. W. Ahl, Dr. Briard, Isaac Kaffenberg.

These are a few of the many. Readers of the HERALD may be surprised to know that the clergy are always well represented, and no sect so well as the Catholics. Not a game passes but there are present about half a dozen Catholic priests, who occupy seats in the pavilion. There is a clergyman — Rev. George A. Groveland from Nashua, N.H. — who, accompanied by his wife or his son, manages to find time to visit the Boston grounds whenever he is in the city and there is a game on the grounds. Rev. Mr. Skinner of Somerville is a constant attendant, and none enjoy the game more. Commissioner Osborn is a constant visitor to the grounds. He generally sits about a dozen seats to the left of Director Conant, and in front row. He, Lieut. Dan Curran of station 10 and Lieut. Spear of the same station see that the police are well represented. Chief Webber of the fire department is often on hand.

Some of the lovers of the game have become converts within a remarkably short time. One of the most striking instances is that of Councilman Isaac Rosnosky. Isaac has become one of the worst of base ball cranks, and the hottest kind of a political fight would have no attractions for him nowadays beside a hot battle for base ball supremacy. He patronizes every game, and when the club is away Music Hall comes in for his attention.

—*Boston Herald*, September 12, 1889: 5.

The Royal Rooters

Red Sox fans follow in the even longer tradition of fanaticism regarding baseball in Boston. One of the reasons, back in 1901, that Ban Johnson and his nascent American League determined to place a franchise in Boston was his awareness of the city's passion for the game. The 1871-75 Boston Red Stockings won four National Association championships in a row and certainly had their fans, and so had the National League's Boston Beaneaters.[3] The Beaneaters (later the Boston Braves) won eight pennants between 1877 and 1898.

Many of the old baseball boosters switched loyalties when the Boston Americans came to town; many others patronized both ballclubs.

Teams had their fans, but there is also a lengthy history of organized fan support, most notably the Royal Rooters in some of Boston baseball's early days. Peter J. Nash, chronicler of the Rooters, traces the history of Boston "cranks" and fans back into the 19th century in his book *Boston's Royal Rooters*.[4] The Rooters organized traveling aggregations which brought 125-130 Boston fans to Baltimore in 1897 to see the Beaneaters beat the Orioles for the National League pennant.

Rooters

The first mention I could find in a Massachusetts newspaper was in the *Boston Herald* of July 21, 1890. In a page 6 article, datelined New York, which contained the sentence, "If there was only one club here all the 'rooters' would know what to do." A little over a year later, the *Springfield Republican* had an article about a game between the Northamptons and the University of Vermonts which talked about scoring three runs in the sixth inning and taking the lead "at which 25 or 20 Northampton 'rooters' went wild."[5]

Nearly another year passed before the *Boston Daily Advertiser* referred to the recent visit of Cap Anson and the Chicago Colts to play the Boston Beaneaters. Boston swept the three-game set, but the Colts had been playing well before arriving, and, anxiously anticipating the arrival of the Colts, "a general feeling of apprehension seized the more timid Boston 'rooters.'"[6]

It was in 1892 that the term seemed to take gradually hold and spread. It was used to describe who we now call "fans" in a *Boston Journal* account of the Harvard/Yale game.[7] On July 17, the *Herald* used "rooters" near the end of an article about two picked nines from the Chamber of Commerce.[8] There were four other usages of the term before the year was done, one each in the *Boston Globe, Journal, Republican,* and *Herald.*[9] The article in the *Globe* used the term in the lead sentence in its coverage of a Boston/New York game: "A small but fervent crowd of Boston rooters occupied the grand stands at the Polo grounds just above the players' bench and watched the battle today."[10] The *Globe* was the first Boston paper to drop the use of quotation marks around the term "rooters." The *Herald* applied it to patrons of a bowling competition.

The word "rooters" began to achieve some currency nationally. Casting a wider net, I found an article (two months earlier in 1890) in the *St. Louis Post-Dispatch* referring to "base ball cranks and rooters at the ball games."[11] In that some month of May 1890, the *Chicago Tribune* carried a mention of "Edward Everett Bell, the ex-Chicagoan and present New York 'rooter' in chief of the Chicago players' team."[12] In July, the *Hartford Courant* noted jovial grocer J. M. Parker as "a constant and earnest 'rooter' for the home team."[13] On April 15 and 16, 1891, the *Washington Post* used the word two days in a row. Understanding and usage was clearly spreading nationally, and no longer requiring the use of quotation marks.

By 1891, the *New York Sun* ran an article entitled "Rooters and Rooting," subtitled, "New Industry Now Recognized In All Sporting Circles. What They Root For, How they Root, and the Result of Their Rooting—They Are Found on the Baseball Field, at the Race Track, in the Gambling-Rooms, and Wherever Games of Chance Are Played—Slang of the New Profession."[14] There was no sense of it being a profession in a business sense, but instead a reflection of passion. The article began, "Rooters and now recognized in all sporting circles. They are the men who have strong feelings for one side or the other in a contest, and encourage their interests and promote their interests is various way. To say a man is rooting is to say he's doing his best for the success of somebody. On the baseball field, for instance, the rooter has his favorite club or his favorite player, for which he shouts, or applauds, or encourages, or bets, or helps along in any way." The article discussed how knowledgeable many rooters are, and then adds that the players had come to see value in the rooters, even blaming defeat on the energetic passions of the crowd: "They could not have won if it had not been for their rooters."

The *Sun* article also noted, "There are many female rooters at all sorts of field sports. They illuminate the grand-stands. They frown on the opposite party. They utter delicate little shouts and sometimes break out in impatient exclamations. They root, and root, and root."

The word achieved widespread acceptance and a mention of "Cincinnati rooters" appears in *Spalding's Base Ball Guide and Official League Book for 1896* on page 12.

Boston Rooters

In the earliest years of the 21st century, it was often observed that Red Sox fans "travel well." It was not uncommon for Red Sox fans to outnumber local Orioles fans at Camden Yards in Baltimore, or Rays fans in Tampa. Even in cities as far from home as Los Angeles, there were organized charter bus trips from, say, Sonny McLean's pub in Santa Monica to Angels Stadium in Anaheim. The team even runs an affiliated enterprise named Red Sox Destinations to take fans on road trips with the Red Sox.

From the beginning, before there even was an American League, Boston's rooters seemed to like to travel. The Boston Beaneaters had won the National League pennant both in 1891 and 1892. Opening Day of the 1893 season was against the Giants at the Polo Grounds in New York, and for the opening ceremonies they took the field first.

Then the Giants were introduced. They were "cheered and cheered," of course, "but were nearly drowned in noise by a crowd of Boston 'rooters' who had come all the way from the Bay State to cheer their men on to victory."[15]

There were individuals who stood out in cities, such as Congressman William Everett from Massachusetts who was profiled in an April 1894 *Globe* article. Everett habitually held a front-row seat in Washington, brought along his private secretary to keep score, and kept up running banter with the players, and was not unknown to yell when he deemed necessary. When Boston came to the capital, he (and his scorer) shared a private box with noted Boston fan "Hi Hi" Dixwell. It was written that he "kept even with the 'Hi Hi' man in amount of noise made."[16]

"Hi Hi" and "Nuf Ced"

There were two "superfans" who stand out in early Boston baseball history—Michael "Nuf Ced" McGreevy and Arthur "Hi Hi" Dixwell. Both became active in the late 1880s and early 1890s.

Dixwell came first. Joanne Hulbert has written a brief biography of Dixwell, with his signature yell, "Hi! Hi!"—his way of expressing his appreciation of a good play. She wrote of the independently wealthy Dixwell, "Besides being considered the greatest baseball crank of them all, he was a director of Boston's Players League club in 1890. He showered his favorite players with gifts of cigars for all when the team won, diamond scarf pins, recliner chairs, loans that often were never paid back, and even an invitation of a European tour to catcher Morgan Murphy. His Dixwell trophy was awarded to the New England League pennant winner. He turned over the ceremonial first shovel of dirt for construction of the Huntington Avenue Grounds when the American League settled into Boston as the new team, threw out the first ball at the first game played there on May 8, 1901, and sent Ban Johnson $100 for season tickets that first year. After the 1903 World's Series win, he presented the Boston club with a lavishly designed pennant flag."[17]

McGreevy was a saloonkeeper from Roxbury, Massachusetts. He followed, explains McGreevy biographer Peter J. Nash, in the footsteps of New York's Nick Engel, who ran a steakhouse and saloon: "A rabid fan of the New York Giants, Engel organized a group of fans known as the High and Mighty Order of Baseball Cranks of Gotham, and also led a contingent of 160 New York fans by train to Baltimore for Opening Day in 1894."[18] So Boston fans weren't the only traveling rooters, but the 1903 World Series cemented Boston's "Royal Rooters" in public consciousness as the pre-eminent band of baseball loyalists. McGreevy established his own watering hole. By 1901, it had become known as the 3rd Base Saloon—with its memorable moniker, the "last stop before home."

The First Rooters Road Trip

The first big Boston rooter road trip came in 1897, in support of the Beaneaters. As Nash put it, "The affinity McGreevy and his followers had for the Boston club culminated in a frenzy of fanatic devotion in September of 1897, when McGreevy organized an army of Boston fans to travel via rail to Baltimore and root for the Beaneaters in what would be the deciding games for the National League pennant. Wearing badges incorporating beanpot themes created by the *Boston Globe* and *Boston Herald* identifying themselves as the "Boston Rooters," the group of nearly 200 fans toured the streets of Baltimore with a hired marching band. Led by Congressman Fitzgerald, the group ended at the Baltimore grounds behind the Boston dugout where McGreevy and the entire Boston contingent rooted on their boys "with horns, rattles and a specially arranged battle-cry."[3] Congressman John F. Fitzgerald was, of course, the famous "Honey Fitz" who grandson John Fitzgerald Kennedy became President of the United States.

There were "fans" by this time; the *Washington Post* had a regular "notes" feature entitled "For the Baseball Fans," which seems to have begun in the spring of 1896. But just as John S. Dooley's daughter Lib Dooley deigned to be called a fan and preferred to be "a friend of the

Red Sox," a rooter was a special breed of fan, not a mere follower of the game but someone who went far above and beyond.

In 1897, as a three-game series in Baltimore loomed on the National League schedule (September 24-27), the *Boston Globe*'s Tim Murnane, himself a former player, wrote that two Bostonians — Billy Rogers and George Appleton — mapped out a round-trip excursion. If they could sign up 100 fans at $25 apiece, they would get them to Baltimore and back. Murnane said, "Nothing would encourage the player more than to have about 100 Boston friends present to see them tear up the earth with the champions. If the rooters take the trip they should carry fish horns and police rattles enough to partially offset the cannonading of that howling Baltimore mob. Even 100 men can make a big noise if properly handled by a good leader."[19] This was, of course, well before the days in which electronic messageboards were thought to be needed to exhort fans to "Make Noise!"

Messrs. Rogers and Appleton got 125 rooters, and the party left downtown Boston at 6:45 PM on September 23. Congressman Fitzgerald was among them, as was McGreevy. Each bore a badge with an enameled brass-bound bar reading "BOSTON ROOTERS" from which hung a piece of silk with an American flag suspended beneath it; attached as well was a miniature medallion. One side of the medallion bore the dates of the road trip, and the other showed a beanpot with the word "Boston" on it, with lightning bolts flashing, the pot being stirred by a representation of "old Satan, politely bowing, hat in hand, as if in mockery of the attempt of the Baltimores to beat the Bostons."[20]

Boston won the first and third of the three-game set, and by season's end had reclaimed the pennant from Baltimore. The Boston rooters had been marked by "unchecked and unconquerable enthusiasm," wrote the *Springfield Republican*, though the *Boston Daily Advertiser* more humbly did say they were such a small part of the vast throng of 25,000 that they "sank into comparative insignificance, but the band played on and the rooters rooted and shouted just the same."[21] Boston won the third game, 19-10, and the *New York Times* wrote, "The visiting 'rooters' own the town tonight. Their brass band is parading through the principal streets and their cry 'Hit her up! Hit her up! Hit her up again! B-O-S-T-O-N' is heard everywhere."[22]

On the evening of October 6, the group of rooters organized and hosted a banquet for the pennant-winning players at Boston's Faneuil Hall. The *Boston Globe*'s subhead dubbed them "Loyal Rooters."[23] It wasn't until a year later, in a brief note on October 3, 1898 (the Beaneaters repeated as league champions), that the newspaper used the phrase "royal rooters," and then only in casual reference to a re-union being planned. The alliteration may have been key to its eventual adoption. (We do find only three earlier references, generic ones in the 1890s, to "royal rooters" in stories about games in Philadelphia, Cincinnati, and Pittsburgh.)

Peter Nash summarized the import of the trip: "As one cohesive cheering unit, McGreevy and his cohorts had successfully transformed themselves into baseball's original 'tenth man.'

"The trip of 1897 laid the groundwork for McGreevy's more formalized contingent that would later become known famously as the Royal Rooters, a group dedicated to traveling and rooting for Ban Johnson's newly organized American League club in Boston that snatched Jimmy Collins and other stars away from the longstanding fan favorite Beaneaters. As noted by *Boston Globe* scribe Tim Murnane, a Royal Rooter sat atop the world of fandom, distinguishing himself as a cut above the lower classes of baseball fans for his willingness to travel on his own dime to root for his club in enemy territory. McGreevy and his men revolutionized the concept."[24]

They also, Nash wrote elsewhere, "introduced fan-orchestrated bands, megaphones, banners, signs, badges, and buttons."[25]

The Beaneaters won the pennant again in 1898, but not again until they were the Boston Braves in 1914. And the championship team of the 1890s was no more. It took the arrival of a brand new team in town to re-energize the populace. Ban Johnson worked with former Beaneaters captain Hugh Duffy in bringing an American League team to Boston in time for an inaugural 1901 season. They recruited star third baseman Jimmy Collins, who in turn brought in Chick Stahl and Buck Freeman, and pitcher Ted Lewis. In the new "baseball war" between the National League and the American League, the three owners of the Nationals, known as the Triumvirs, came up short in the eyes of the public, particularly as the Boston Americans had success on the diamond. As Harold Kaese put it, "The Triumvirs had become symbols of stinginess. In saloons and on streetcorners they were ridiculed by fans who took their cue from the newspaper writers. The South End ball park was an ugly little wart. Players were known to be dissatisfied with their small salaries. The smug attitude with which the Triumvirs regarded the new intruders cost them friends."[26]

Hi Hi Dixwell turned the first shovelful of dirt for the construction of the Boston American League's Huntington Avenue Grounds ballpark. Nuf Ced McGreevy and Tim Murnane were both at the ceremony as well. Known initially as simply the Boston Americans, this is the team which became known as the Boston Red Sox in December 1907.

Jimmy Collins also brought in other players, such as Cy Young, who went 33-10 in the team's first season.

It also helped the team's immediate appeal that bleacher seats could be had for 25 cents, and in a brand new ballpark, for half the price charged by the "smug" National League team. And they won games, too, competing with the Chicago White Sox to finish in second place, just four games behind, while the Beaneaters finished in fifth place, a discouraging 20 ½ games out of first place.

Boston baseball fandom rather quickly shifted its allegiance to the new team, the Americans. For Opening Day at the Huntington Avenue Grounds, Arthur Dixwell threw out the ceremonial first ball and on May 9 a *Boston Globe* headline proclaimed success: "American League Men Given Royal Welcome By 11,500 Rooters."

As early as June 9, just over 30 games into the season, the *Worcester Daily Spy* opined, "The Boston American League team is just now the only bidder for patronage in the centre of civilization, and the cultured rooters are certainly turning out for the Collins brigade."[27]

By season's end, the Americans had drawn 289,448 (ranking second among the eight AL clubs). The Beaneaters attracted 146,502 paying patrons, just more than half as many, ranking last among all eight National League teams.

McGreevy was said to be putting together a road trip to Philadelphia in September 1902 for four games from the 19th through the 22nd. If it came to pass, there was no mention readily found in the *Globe* or *Herald.*

The Rooters were fully behind the Collinsmen when they won the American League pennant in 1903 and a sizable party traveled to Pittsburgh for the four games played there during the 1903 World Series. This was the first World Series ever held. It was in Pittsburgh that they famously truly launched the first Boston victory anthem, "Tessie." They hired bands to play the song—incessantly, so much so that some of the Pirates remembered years later how the constant playing unnerved them.

About 125 Royal Rooters (they also dubbed themselves the "Invaders" for this trip), took the train from Boston's South Station to Pittsburgh on October 4. The scheduled October 5 game was rained out, but the *Boston Herald* noted, "The rooters are wearing badges ... made of red silk with a gold pin on top and the following inscription is printed across it: 'Boston American League Rooters, 1903.' ... if music and cheering will help, any these loyal rooters will pull Boston out on top."[28] The initial day's cheering didn't help enough; Boston came up on the short end, 5-4, and were down three games to one in the best-of-five "World's Series." Boston had rallied in the ninth, falling just one run short, but the rally gave the rooters new life.

Then came "Tessie." The song was a popular Broadway song of the day. Tom Burton of the Rooters found some sheet music at a Pittsburgh music store and the Rooters wrote parodied lyrics to "Tessie," which they had printed up and distributed. They hired a 50-piece Italian band and raised a ruckus. Immediately, and ever afterward, they felt the music had spurred on their players. Starting the following day, they had the band play "Tessie" over and over, and over again. Some of the lyrics of the parody give us the flavor:

Honus, why do you hit so badly?
Take a back seat and sit down
Honus, at bat you look so sadly
Hey, why don't you get out of town?

After delivering the final line, the Rooters stomped their feet loudly three times, shouting "Bang! Bang! Bang!" and then singing the line again. The *Boston Post* said they were like "howling maniacs" and historian Roger Abrams said that Pittsburgh owner Barney Dreyfuss "ordered supporting beams erected under Section J, lest the Royal Rooters' 'frenzied enthusiasm' break down the park's grandstand."[29]

The following day, they won, 11-2. The *Pittsburgh Gazette* wrote, "At the conclusion of the game the Boston rooters were almost wild with joy, and headed by a band, they danced about the grandstand and sang 'Tessie' until they were blue in the face."

After the Bostons had taken a four games to three lead, and returned home from Pittsburgh, player/manager Jimmy Collins credited the Rooters. "The support given the team by the 'Loyal Rooters' will never be forgotten. They backed us up as only Bostonians could, and no little portion of our success is due to this selfsame band of enthusiasts. Noise—why, they astonished all Pittsburg with their enthusiasm."[30]

The Boston Americans won four games in a row, and the 1903 World Series, and many felt the organized, vocal, and energetic support of the Royal Rooters had made a difference.

As Lawrence Ritter wrote, "They played it so often and delivered it with such vigor—incessantly, relentlessly, *ad nauseam*—that it began to take its toll on the opposition. Even decades later, Pittsburgh's third baseman Tommy Leach said, "I think those Boston fans won the Series…We beat them three out of four games, and then they started singing that damn Tessie song…Sort of got on your nerves after a while. And before we knew what happened, we'd lost the Series.'"[31]

In 1904, the pennant race went down to the wire between Boston and the New York Highlanders (later named the Yankees). Charlie Lavis and Mike McGreevy led the Rooters to see the final October 10 doubleheader in New York; one win would secure the pennant.

A photograph shows them maybe 100 strong, parading up 165th Street behind a pair of 20-foot banners proclaiming "BOSTON ROOTERS." Among the more noteworthy leaders, again, were "Nuf Ced" McGreevy and "Honey Fitz." Active throughout was Lib Dooley's father John S. Dooley. (Lib Dooley was, in her own words, a "friend of the Red Sox." She died in the year 2000. Later that day, the Sox lost to the New York Yankees, 22-1. She was not a fan, she emphasized. "A fan leaves in the seventh inning. I have always considered myself a friend of not only the Red Sox but the whole game. Being a friend means being there from the 'Star Spangled Banner' to the final out."[32])

The *Boston Herald* credited the Rooters in a front-page subhead: "ROYAL ROOTERS GREAT HELP." Again, they hired a band. Jerry Watson stood on the roof of the Boston bench and led the band, playing "Tessie" over and over again "until the performers must have been as tired of the auditors, some of whom inquired innocently enough if that was the only air the band could play." The paper continued, "Well, Tessie was on deck as she was in Pittsburg. The rooters sang and yelled and howled and cheered until they had little left in the shape of a voice."[33]

The Bostons beat the Highlanders to win the 1904 American League pennant, but the National League champion New York Giants refused to play them in the World Series, still carrying on their own war against the American League (but maybe also fearful of losing to them, and thus losing their own self-image as the best team in the land.)

In both 1903 and 1904, the Boston Rooters held a ball with a concert and dancing at Union Park Hall in December. About 700 persons attended the 1904 ball.

It wasn't only the 1903 Pirates who became irritated at times with rooters. Fans in other cities adopted this new form with energy, and I. E. Sanborn of the *Chicago Tribune* finally issued a blistering broadside early in 1908. The Cubs had won the 1907 World Series (which had resumed in 1905). Sanborn complained, "Chicago's interest in the world champions, present, past, and prospective, is being distracted by its rooters' clubs, which apparently are bent on butting into the limelit baseball stage at the opening of a pennant campaign and staying there to share the attention and applause which hitherto have been given the players." He said "the baseball public won't stand for it," acknowledging that "these organized rooting associations or clubs are something of an innovation, still in their infancy comparatively" but that the evidence was in that "the play's the thing" and that "no sideshows are wanted."

Sanborn noted the White Sox Rooters association raising money to hire bands for the season, and the West Side Rooters' Social Club having done the same to organize rooting for the Cubs. He asserted that the din-making of the "bands of frenzied rooters, each striving to outdo the other" was distasteful to any sane fan. The story is worth a read.[34]

McGreevy traveled to spring training every year, even traveling all the way to Redondo Beach, California for the remarkable 1911 spring training tour.[35] A lover of baseball itself, there were other excursions he organized, including one later in 1911 to see the Philadelphia Athletics play the New York Giants in the 1911 World Series, but for the Red Sox there wasn't a whole lot to cheer about until 1912. Nor was there for the Braves until 1914.

When the Red Sox won the pennant in 1912, the Rooters reappeared on the scene in good numbers. Some 300 "Red Sox Rooters" took a special train to New York on October 7 to see the Sox take on the Giants. They met some opposition. "After Game One, the automobiles of the Royal Rooters were 'stoned and deluged with dirt by the urchins lined up along the streets and avenues.' After Game Four, 'it was the automobiles occupied by the players that were bombarded and many of the occupants suffered from dirt being thrown.' Fortunately, there were no serious injuries despite 'some of the oldest of the hoodlums being particularly good marksmen.' Buck O'Brien was hit in the face by a sharp stone that cut the skin...The Red Sox complained that New York's finest stood by without intervening."[36]

It was again a best-of-nine Series. Game Seven, at Fenway Park, was most discouraging, and created a rupture between Red Sox management and its most fervent organized fans. The Royal Rooters paraded around, and then entered the ballpark behind their "Boston Royal Rooters" banner, only to find there had been a blunder. "Red Sox management had sold the tickets routinely held for the team's booster club, the Royal Rooters, and the 300-strong troupe paraded into the park only to find their seats taken....[T]here was a lot of pushing and shoving on the field with five mounted policemen having to push back the team's most loyal fans. The Rooters felt aggrieved and many joined in booing Red Sox management in a demonstration after the game that even resulted in loud cheers for the New York owners who had reserved a special section for them while at the Polo Grounds. Most boycotted the ballclub the following day. It was no coincidence that about 40 percent of the park was devoid of fans on the 16th, even though it was the final game of the championship."[37]

Even in 1913, the memory rankled. Fans of Boston baseball, the Rooters jumped behind the "Miracle Braves" in 1914, the team which had been in last place as late in the season as July 18 — but rallied and won the pennant. Some 200 members of the Rooters, including former Boston Mayor John "Honey Fitz" Fitzgerald, traveled to Philadelphia to support the Braves in the World Series. The Braves swept the Philadelphia Athletics in four games, playing the final two at Fenway Park, the better to accommodate larger crowds than the Braves' own South End Grounds.

In 1915, it was Philadelphia versus Boston again in the World Series, but this time it was the Red Sox versus the Phillies. Once more, the Boston team prevailed. This time, the games were played at brand-new Braves Field, which was now the larger of the two ballparks. On

October 7, some 350 of the "royalest, loyalest, noisiest rooters that ever left Boston" entrained for New York, and then Philadelphia.[38] After losing the first game, the Red Sox won the next three games by identical 2-1 scores and then the first and final game, 5-4.

Come 1916, the Red Sox repeated, again winning the American League pennant. This time their opponents were the Brooklyn Robins. They won Game One in Boston, and Game Two in 14 innings (a complete game effort by pitcher Babe Ruth). About 300 Brooklyn Boosters had some to Boston to see Game Two. Nerves were frayed as the game continued on. "At one point in the bottom of the 11th, the band was playing 'Tessie' so incessantly that the Robins took the unusual step of complaining, even threatening to deny the Royal Rooters entry into Ebbets Field if they didn't stop. Plate umpire Bill Dinneen actually ordered the band to stop playing, a bit ironic in that Dinneen had been on the 1903 Boston team that won the first World Series in part thanks to the 'Tessie' rally song." The *Boston Globe* said that once owner Charles Ebbets himself had protested, the music had ceased. Some Sox partisans asked why the Brooklyn Boosters had nonetheless been permitted "to beat their dish-pan accompaniment while Boston was at bat Saturday and again yesterday."[39] The Red Sox won the 1916 Series, again in five games, dropping only Game Three.

In 1918, the Red Sox famously won their last World Series for 86 years, then had to wait until 2004 to win another. Fans in the interim were born, lived their lives, and died. All the games were played in September, the season curtailed because of the first world war. The first three games of the 1918 Series were held in Chicago. Boston won two and the Cubs won one. Then the Series came to Boston. Perhaps because of the war, there wasn't the frenzy that had characterized earlier years. The Royal Rooters were reported to be "quietly organizing" prior to Game Four; this was not an organization which had previously been associated with anything akin to quiet. The Red Sox honored a group of 30 wounded veterans prior to the game. Neither the games in Chicago nor Boston were sold out. Only 22,183 were at Fenway for Game Four. Game Five drew over 24,000, but the final, decisive Game Six only attracted 15,238. John J. Hallahan wrote in the *Herald* that "the cloud that is hanging over this country by the bigger and more serious game being fought on the other side was reflected in the attendance."[40] Game Five had been delayed after the players learned that their compensation was being cut by nearly 50%, and they threatened not to play. They were cajoled into it by promises made. One of the reasons Game Six may have attracted such a small crowd was due to uncertainty whether the game itself would be played.[41] It was, and the Red Sox won, but this wasn't a year for the brash boosterism of the Royal Rooters. The Red Sox didn't clinch another World Championship at home until 2013.

Bob Ryan of the *Boston Globe* once wrote, "The famed Royal Rooters came into being in the 1890s. They traveled to Pittsburgh during the 1903 World Series and raised holy hell. They were the BoSox Club, only they drank more."[42]

Let us pause here, backing up to some extent, and look at another organization that had developed in Boston.

The Winter League

When not at the games—such as during the fallow months known as the offseason—fans organized a series of booster clubs to host dinners and the like. Over the course of time, these booster clubs went by various names such as the Winter League, the Half Century Club, the BoSox Club, the BLOHARDS, and the Bluenose BoSox Brotherhood.

Overlapping in time with the Royal Rooters, the first of these outside-the-park Boston baseball booster clubs was the Winter League. They supported both the National League and American League aggregations. The first mention we have found of the Winter League comes in 1908, when the group is said to have held its annual outing at Sunset Farm in Holliston, Massachusetts. That this was already considered to be annual event suggests there were earlier evenings as well. John Campbell was president, and John S. Dooley the vice president and secretary. Members of the organization included Red Sox owner John I. Taylor, former ballplayer and *Boston Globe* sportswriter Tim Murnane, former players Hugh Duffy and Tom McCarthy, as well as a number of Boston area businessmen.[43]

What was then called the winter league is what folks for years have dubbed the "hot stove league"—a chance for people to get together and talk about baseball in the off-season. John Dooley was not only noted as vice president and secretary of the Winter League, but prized for his drive to build the organization. He'd been the first president and, apparently, the principal organizer as well. An appreciation in a January 1913 issue of the *Boston Journal* referred to "Jack Dooley, secretary of the Winter League Club, by whose efforts the club has nearly doubled its membership in the last six months…." was awarded a diamond ring in recognition of his work. The 1913 dinner honored Hughie Jennings, who pronounced that he'd enjoyed the "time of his life."[44]

John Dooley had so many interesting connections with the Red Sox that we want to take considerable time to look at his life and his love of baseball here.

Dooley's involvement precedes the Red Sox, helping get the franchise settled and into its first ballpark in Boston, and rooting for Boston baseball teams without missing an Opening Day for three-quarters of a century. According to Jack Mahoney's article in the April 14, 1968 *Boston Herald*, Dooley had seen every opener since 1882. Art Ballou's article in the June 20, 1963 *Globe* dated his Opening Day streak back to 1894 — and Dooley added that there were many seasons in which he'd seen every home game. Whichever date one picks, by 1968 he'd been to at least 75 in a row.[45]

John S. Dooley

John Stephen Dooley was born in Somerville, Massachusetts on Christmas Day, 1873. He lived to the age of 96, dying on March 1, 1970.

From a very early age, Dooley had a connection to the game of baseball and as Americans began to orbit in space, he was able to tell people that he had witnessed the very first baseball game ever played under the lights. That newfangled invention the Weston light bulb was but three years old (Edison's first incandescent bulb was invented in 1879) when the first night game was played at Hull, Massachusetts on September 2, 1880. The next day's Boston newspapers tell the story of how two teams from competing Boston department stores (Jordan Marsh Co. and R. H. White & Co.) played a full nine innings in Hull under "a new system of electric lighting" at Strawberry Hill, on the grounds of the Sea Foam House at Nantasket Beach. Three large wooden towers, each 100 feet high, were erected and placed some 500 feet apart. On the top of each were placed 12 "Weston lamps," each grouping providing some 30,000 candlepower of illumination. The system of massed groupings of lights was provided by the Northern Electric Light Company. A 30-horsepower generator powered the array.

The *Boston Post* explained that "on the broad lawn in the rear of the house there was sufficient light to enable a game of base ball to be played, though scarcely [with] the precision as by daylight." The two picked nines squared off, the game tied 16-16 after nine innings and called off so the players could catch the last boat back to Boston. The *Boston Herald* compared the light to that of "the moon at its full" and said that as a result "the batting was weak and the pitchers were poorly supported." And young Jack Dooley was there. His half-brother William Dooley worked for R. H. White and had taken his younger brother to the event.

Dooley was a pitcher himself in his younger days, playing for the Franklins of Egleston Square, according to a May 13, 1956 article in the *Boston Sunday Post*. He also played some semipro ball in Attleboro and made another acquaintance in the process, Chick McLaughlin, captain of the Harvard baseball team. Through McLaughlin, he met Joe Kennedy, who he recalled as "a first baseman, but not too good." Kennedy "played only one game—the last one against Yale—and then only the last two innings to get his letter. But he played for Chick's college all-stars which toured the area after the college season was over. Through my acquaintance with Joe, I met young Jack." Yes, that Jack Kennedy.

In fact, Dooley knew a couple of Boston's major political figures. As a young man growing up in Roxbury, Jack Dooley used to deliver milk on Eustis Street together with a young John Michael Curley. When William Dooley died, Curley was a pallbearer at his funeral. The Dooleys had a summer home in Hull on B Street, just a few houses away from where Joseph P. Kennedy had a home. Honey Fitz had a home in Hull, too.

Not surprisingly, Dooley frequented ballgames of Boston's only team, the Nationals, who played in the late 19th century at the Walpole Street Grounds and, later, the South End Grounds. Dooley recalled visiting the clubhouse in that era, one when "the players had to wait in line for a bath in a flat tin tub. It took them longer to get the bath over than the playing of the game itself."[46]

Dooley was one of the men to whom Connie Mack turned when Ban Johnson enlisted his help in creating the American League. And Johnson knew Dooley well. Dooley told the *Boston Globe*'s Art Ballou in 1963 that the architect of the American League used to call him "my little Irishman from Boston."

The story, as Dooley set it down, went thus: In the fall of 1900, Johnson came to Boston to see if it were feasible to situate a charter American League franchise in a city already known for its passionate interest in baseball. He set up shop in the Old South building on Washington Street and sought out Hugh Duffy, holding a number of meetings with him. Dooley sat in on a few of the meetings. Lining up the players was easier than finding a suitable location for the ballpark. Duffy had considered a position as a principal with a proposed American Association team to be placed in the area in an attempt to fend off an American League incursion. Duffy declined, arguing, "The grounds are too far out. They are in Cambridge and will not draw from Boston. Harvard students might patronize the club, but that is about all."

"I recall Peter Kelley, an old newspaper man, calling on me at my office," Dooley wrote in a brief account he typed up. Kelley was calling on behalf of Cleveland's Charles Somers, designated as the first president of the Boston American League club. Kelley himself "had an option on the old bicycle track across the Charles River in Cambridge, on a lease calling for a yearly rental of $5,000." Johnson, though, didn't like the Cambridge location recommended by Mack and Clark Griffith. He didn't want a Boston team playing anywhere but in Boston. He kept that information to himself and the small circle of men trying to help situate the team.

Boston was the eighth and final city selected as home for a club in the new American League. Only by finding an appropriate site for a baseball field would the American League truly decide to place a team in Boston. Had the men not found a good location, the league would have placed its eighth club in either Buffalo or Indianapolis. SABR researcher Doug Pappas found that the National League's Arthur Irwin had leased the Cambridge property in a pre-emptive move to try and keep out the upstart league, but the lease was structured such that it would expire if the property was sold.

A location deemed more suitable, however, was a site on Huntington Avenue controlled by the Boston Elevated Railway Company. Duffy showed the site to Kelley and they both recommended it to Johnson. Dooley recalled Durand Associates as the actual owners of the land, but they had leased it to the railway, which envisioned building a terminal there. The car barn wasn't in the cards, but the railway was holding out for a $10,000 a year rental.

Dooley was at the time working for the firm of J. R. Prendergast, brokers in cotton goods and yarn with offices at 87 Milk Street.

Prendergast's brother Daniel was in charge of the real estate department of the Boston Elevated. Dooley knew the terminal plan was off—it turned out there was an ordinance that prevented the construction of car barns on the land which, even though it had served as a dump, was still across the street from the opera house—and urged Duffy and Kelley to approach Dan Prendergast, offer $5,000 a year "and mention my name. Under no conditions, I said, were they to go higher than $5,000."

The offer was, Dooley said, "violently refused" and Prendergast called Dooley to complain about the "measly rental" the men had offered. "If you want my advice," Dooley says he told Prendergast, "I'd grab that $5,000 offer because they can get that wonderful site in Cambridge for that figure. You'd better grab them right now before they close with Cambridge."

Prendergast took the bit and a deal was struck. Dooley later told the *Boston Post*'s Gerry Hern, "I suppose I should be a little sorry for what I did to get the American League in here, but when I sit in Fenway Park these days, I figure maybe the good Lord will forgive me. It was in a good cause."

In 1956, Gerry Hern of the *Boston Post* wrote, "More than anyone, Jack Dooley is responsible for the American League obtaining the Huntington Ave. grounds as their playing field." Had Dooley not helped out, there might never have been a Boston Red Sox. The February 2, 1901 issue of *The Sporting News* records the formal awarding of a Boston franchise to Somers. Three weeks later, the February 23 *Sporting Life* reported that Somers had said the American League would never have invaded Boston if the National League had acceded to its original request for recognition as a major league.

Dooley later went to work for his brother at Wm. J. Dooley & Co., 60 Congress Street. Like Prendergast's, the firm was also a broker in cotton goods and cotton yarns, and did quite a good business at the time serving the mills of New England. Later, in 1912, William Dooley was honored by Pope Pius X, who bestowed on him the title of Knight of the Sword and Cape, carrying the rank of private chamberlain to the Holy Father. At the same time, James Prendergast was made Grand Commander of the Order of St. Gregory.

Soon after the AL franchise was established, the 1903 team won the pennant and Dooley was there in the grandstand watching the first World Series game ever played on October 1, a member of the Royal Rooters. The following year, Boston won the pennant again, playing the final two games against the New York Highlanders. Dooley was there, too. One finds his name in the October 9, 1904 *Globe*, listed among the Rooters who took two train cars from Boston to see those last two games.

The Winter League, Dooley once said, was organized with a simple purpose: "Its object is to promote better baseball for Boston. In its membership are listed a large number of Boston's royal rooters—most of them daily attendants at the game." Dooley himself didn't just make Opening Day. There were many years in which he never missed a game—and that often meant taking in games with both of Boston's teams. For decades, he made the annual pilgrimage to spring training as well.

The Winter League Club, as it was often called, met with some frequency. Boston newspapers report both a dinner in Holliston to honor Hughie Jennings and a night at the Majestic Theatre in January 1913, a dinner at the Hotel Lenox in April, a trip to Portland in May for the opening game of the New England League season there, a trip to Fitchburg in January 1914, and a February dinner at Hurlburt's Hotel honoring Johnny Evers. Dooley and Hugh Duffy were noted as traveling back from a February meeting in New York, and Dooley and several others including Duffy traveled to New York again with the Braves late in September. In December 1914, he began organizing a winter dinner to honor Braves manager George Stallings. Late in the month was "Maranville Night" at the Old Howard Theatre; the *Globe* noted that "Jack Dooley and his Winter League will be on hand." He was spotted in the corridors at meetings of New England League baseball in January 1915 and at a Quincy House dinner where the 125 dined on turkeys sent from Stallings' plantation in Georgia. Dooley was described as the "moving spirit of the Winter League."

He turned up again, involved at an old-time athletes' event in Holliston in July. The annual feast was held at Quincy House in February 1916, attended by 150 members. That December, President Dooley announced the annual banquet, this time to honor Rabbit Maranville, who became a longtime friend of the family (when he married, John's wife Winifred Dooley gave the Maranvilles the baby carriage that had held Lib Dooley as an infant).

Dooley continued to play some ball for the enjoyment of it. A 1912 article in the *Boston Post* has him playing third base on the same Winter Club team as two future Hall of Famers (the Hall of Fame wasn't founded for another 20 years). Hugh Duffy played center field and Tom McCarthy played left. Other players known in old-time Boston baseball circles included Jack Barry, Arthur Cooper, Carl Nichols, and Jack Slattery. Both Barry (beginning in 1915) and Slattery (back in 1901, the first year of the franchise, before they were the Red Sox) played for the Red Sox, and Cooper was scouting for the Sox at the time.

The following April, Dooley managed a Winter League team "composed of a number of old-timers, college and semi-professional stars" to play against Hugh Duffy's Portland team of the New England League. Nichols and Slattery were Dooley's choice of batterymates, and Walter Lonergan (1911 Red Sox) and "Chick" McLaughlin were set for the infield. In April 1914, a brief note says that Dooley, president of the Winter League, had umpired a game in Fitchburg between that New England League team and the Boston Pilgrims, "a team composed of former college players." Dooley was "struck by a foul ball behind the right ear, and it was badly lacerated."

That didn't dampen John Dooley's fervor. Dooley had the passion to organize. In July 1914, he was back at Sunset Farm and joined in the founding of the Old Time Athletes' Association. Dooley is listed as on the original board of directors. It was apparently not a charitable organization to take care of elderly ballplayers, but instead one to "bring together men for a few more desperate flings at athletic glory," in the words of Joanne Hulbert. Joanne points out that Sunset Farm still exists today with a street address of 320 Chamberlain Street, in the section of Holliston known as—this is for real—Mudville.

In May 1918, Rabbit Maranville, Del Gainer, Mike McNally, Whitey Witt, Herb Pennock, and Leo Callahan—all in the U.S. Navy—set sail under sealed orders, among those who saw them off were John Dooley and former Red Sox manager Jack Barry, now a Chief Yeoman in the Navy himself.

It should be no surprise that when it came time to campaign for Sunday baseball in Massachusetts, John Dooley was in the midst of it, along with his brother-in-law Eugene J. O'Connor. A catcher in his early days, O'Connor played for the Boston Brotherhood Club and the Boston team in the United States League. He was apparently signed by the Boston Nationals at one point but does not appear to have played in a major league game. He covered baseball for the *Boston American* and became sports editor of the paper in 1904. His November 9, 1952 *Boston Globe* obituary deemed him "one of the original advocates of Sunday baseball and also was credited with bringing about twilight baseball." An appreciation written several days later by Victor O. Jones was headlined "Father of Sunday Baseball."

With a six-day workweek typical at the time, there were precious few times that workingmen could take in a baseball game. O'Connor was willing to go to great lengths to help extend baseball's popularity, even though that meant coming up against the Lord's Day laws of the period with a little civil disobedience. The October 21, 1912 *Globe* tells how O'Connor got himself arrested by playing baseball on Boston Common on Sunday afternoon the day before.

The fight dragged on for years, Sunday baseball not becoming legal until the 1929 season. A more complete story of Boston Sunday baseball is told in *Red Sox Threads*, but we want to underscore here the role that John Dooley played in allowing Sunday baseball to be played at Fenway Park. Dooley reportedly urged an attorney friend of his, Charles Young of Quincy, to approach Lt. Gov. Leverett Saltonstall, to see what could be done regarding the prohibition against a baseball game being held within 100 yards of the Church of the Disciples. Saltonstall visited the minister, who had no objection at all and since 1932, the way has been cleared for Sunday games at Fenway.

In 1951, the *Boston Sport-Light* had Dooley as secretary of the Sarasota Athletic Club and presented a testimonial to Joe Cronin at their annual gathering. It seems he was active organizing in Florida as well.

Mr. Dooley's son, John S. Dooley, Jr., served as manager of the Boston College baseball team in 1926. He was a shortstop, but his son John J. Dooley says that he chose not to play baseball in college so he could concentrate on his studies. John J., grandson to our man, worked as a professional baseball umpire from 1978 to 2000 after completing a career in the United States Navy.

The Bull Pen A.C.

During the World War II years, the Bull Pen A.C. was an organization of bleacherites that was strong enough to have hosted annual dinners at the swank Parker House. Apparently it began in 1941, since its fifth annual dinner was held on September 22, 1945. Two hundred came to the event. Elmer Foote was the M. C. and the "swoon singer" Kid Parker entertained. The group honored Red Sox reliever Mike Ryba, presenting him with a check for $500 (which was reportedly matched by Sox GM Eddie Collins.)[47] The group survived the war, and its sixth annual event was held at the Parker House on September 24, 1946. Foote was the emcee again, and Gov. Maurice Tobin was the principal speaker. Six Red Sox players were presented traveling bags: Mace Brown, Dom DiMaggio, Joe Dobson, Bobby Doerr, Dave Ferriss, and Ryba. Three other Red Sox players attended. A note in the February 3, 1947 *Boston Traveler* naming the club's president, Sen. Foote, said the club would be glad to know that charter member Ryba had taken a position as player/manager with the Lynn team of the New England League. When Ryba died of a fall in 1971, the Club was noted in a story of appreciation which mentioned John Carr and Bugs Murphy among other leaders of the club and noted that it had "never thrown a party for Ted Williams, Lefty Grove, or Jimmy Foxx, but it threw one for Mike Ryba."[48]

We the People Speak, the "Sun Bums," or simply "The Bleacherites"

This was almost certainly the same group as The Bull Pen A.C. It was either known by a couple of different names, or was coincidentally drawing from the same constituency at the same time, one of "noted figures in law, medicine, business, and what-have-you." One account called the apparently short-lived club "We the People Speak." The group was described in news accounts in almost the same terms as the Bull Pen A.C.—as "an organization of bleacherites at Fenway Park" which began in 1942 (the September 24, 1942 *Herald* referred to them as The Bleacherites," and noted 200 coming to dinner at the Parker House.) The *Globe* named Foote as a leader. Joe Dobson and Mike Ryba were honored. On September 7, 1944, they, too, held an annual gathering at Boston's Parker House, reported as their third. Guests included Pete Fox, Bob Johnson, and Mike Ryba. In 1967, as the founding of the BoSox Club was announced, Harold Kaese recalled them as the "Sun Bums," naming both Foote and Spider Murphy.[49]

The Lido Beachcombers A.C., or the Sarasota Athletic Club

The Lido Beachcombers A.C. was yet another Red Sox fan club, also referred to as the Sarasota Athletic Club. Some of its Cambridge members were depicted in a *Boston American* photograph which ran on February 17, 1953, as they bid farewell to Dom DiMaggio on his way to spring training. That June they held a dinner in East Boston to honor Billy Consolo, Milt Bolling, and Gene Stephens. They were described as "composed of royal rooters who follow the Red Sox to Sarasota."[50] An article in the December 15, 1954 *Sporting News* mentions the dinner given for Sam Mele, a "welcome home" party at the Fresh Pond Grill in Cambridge in early December after he was reacquired by the Red Sox. GM Joe Cronin and Johnny Pesky were guests as well. The Beachcombers were referred to as "fans and writers who visit Sarasota when the Sox are training in Florida." It was apparently a loose-knit aggregation. The dinner was chaired by Bill Gianelli of Cambridge, "chairman of the arrangements committee."[51]

The Red Sox One Half Century Club

Some years after the Red Sox passed their 50th anniversary, apparently in 1961, a group of boosters formed the Red Sox One Half Century Club. The first honorary president? John S. Dooley. The *Boston Globe* called it "the new club of old Red Sox fans" and noted the honor of Dooley as "the man who helped find a place for them to play on Huntington av. in 1901."[52] Their third annual dinner was held on September 22, 1963. The club received a flurry of attention in the years Johnny Pesky managed the Red Sox, with John Dooley appearing in a sports page cartoon in the *Herald* and with Dooley being presented a silver cup at the 1963 event, at Fenway. Photographs from 1963 and 1965 show Dooley with Pesky, Bobby Doerr, Mel Parnell, Duffy Lewis, writers John Drohan and Jack Malaney, and fellow booster Dick Casey. In September 1966, the Club honored Duffy Lewis at a dinner again held at Fenway Park. "It isn't a big organization," noted the *Globe*, "just a group of guys who get along in years and like to meet once in a while." Bernard P. "Dick" Casey and John Drohan of the *Traveler* were among the leaders.[53] Drohan became president in 1964. Duffy Lewis was named honorary president in 1966.

The Half Century Club overlapped briefly with the BoSox Club. A March 1968 note in the *Globe* said that Duffy Lewis was being honored in Milwaukee (he'd been traveling secretary of the Boston, and then Milwaukee, Braves) for his 80th birthday in April. Lewis would travel from his home in Salem, New Hampshire for the event, and it was said that Dick Casey "will represent the Red Sox Half Century Club at the festivities."[54]

Soon after the BoSox Club was announced, columnist John Gillooly of the *Record American*, wrote that the Red Sox now had "two (2) booster clubs, the Bosox and the Half-Century Club," adding, "I have one word...merge."[55]

The Boston Braves

The mention of the Boston Braves, of course, recognizes the National League franchise that operated in Boston from 1871 (as the Boston Red Stockings) through the 1952 season, moving to Milwaukee in March 1953.

Bob Brady, President of the Boston Braves Historical Association, offered thoughts in July 2016. He wrote, "One might offer that there was a Depression Era 'seed' from which the BoSox Club might have germinated. Perhaps the Braves' Knot Hole Gang, inaugurated by Judge Fuchs, deserves an 'honorable mention.' There are still a few surviving 'gang' members around who retain a fierce loyalty to the Boston Braves because of that program.

"In the mid '40's upon the dawning of the 'Three Little Steam Shovels' era of Boston Braves ownership and through the creative efforts of Director of Public Relations Bill Sullivan attempts were made to encourage the formation of 'Booster's Clubs.' In a letter dated March, 1947 from General Manager John J. Quinn, the last paragraph read:

Quite a number of Braves' fans have expressed a desire to form Booster's Clubs in the various cities and towns within range of our field. If anyone who reads this letter is desirous of organizing a club in his city we surely will be more than pleased to cooperate in making such a club successful. Therefore, if you might be thinking in terms of a Booster's organization write and we will give you full coopera-tion. Needless to say, you would be helping the Braves, and we would be mindful of this assistance."[56]

Bob added further thoughts: "Both the Braves and the Red Sox fostered such boosterism through club fan newspapers during this era, the *Braves Bulletin* and *Red Sox Ramblings*, respectively. In addition, the Braves were the first major-league team to produce promotional films— *Take Me Out To The Wigwam* in 1946 (B&W) and *The Braves Family* in 1947 (the first such film produced in glorious color!). These films were shown throughout New England at gatherings such as 'smokers' and pre-season 'hot stove league' events. According to a piece in a *Braves Bulletin*, 'more than 200 clubs' had booked *Take Me Out To The Wigwam*. In the absence of an exclusive club dedicated to your favorite team, these gatherings provided a limited outlet to adult and youth baseball fans until something more specifically dedicated came along like the BoSox Club. Another way that the Tribe and Red Sox aligned themselves with organizations was through the encouragement and support/sponsorship of pre-game tributes/festivities toward home and visiting team ballplayers with local ties. E.g., in 1946 the Braves parlayed with its Merrimack Valley fans to welcome Lowell native and Pirates outfielder Johnny Barrett. Cambridge fans were accommodated when they planned a night for the Cubs' Eddie Waitkus. Likewise, Milford fans once honored native son Hank Camelli. With the kick-off of night baseball at Braves Field, the club's promotion department sprang into action and would send representatives to local groups, clubs and organizations and make the necessary arrangements for bus transportation and reserved seating. The Braves specifically targeted Lowell, Lawrence, Haverhill, Lynn, Salem, Fall River, Taunton, Brockton, Wakefield, Melrose, Reading, Norwood, Winchester, and Quincy with such efforts. American Legion posts were another target of such boosterism campaigns.

"Cultivation of the female fan was a hallmark of both of Boston's ball clubs. In addition to Ladies Days promotions, rabid distaff side followers like Lolly Hopkins and her 'girls' were very visible at the ballparks and were popular with ballplayers and management alike. Lolly was featured in a Braves promotional film and was called upon during fan appreciation giveaways to draw prize winners."[57]

The BoSox Club
— First Look

The Half Century Club seemed to fade very quickly afterward, because when Quincy's Ken Coleman first arrived in Boston to broadcast Red Sox baseball in 1966, he was unaware of any recognized booster club. Ken came back home to his native Boston, having worked in Cleveland for several years. While broadcasting for the Indians, he'd been a member of the Wahoo Club. "It was an Indians booster club," he told this author, "and when I came to Boston I spoke with Bill Crowley, who was the public relations director of the Red Sox."[58] He told Crowley about the Wahoo Club and got Cleveland's Gabe Paul and Al Rosen on a speaker phone to talk with Crowley and some other interested people in Boston. They described the club and how it worked. Coleman says it was quite a small club at the time, sometimes only a dozen or two members coming to gatherings.

His initial impetus inspired a group of Red Sox fans—some "50 prominent Boston businessmen"—to organize the BoSox Club and it had its first meeting in early 1967—and what a year that kicked off! The club's first event was a "Welcome Home to the Red Sox" luncheon held on April 10 at Anthony's Pier Four, the day before the home opener. Some 260 members and their guests attended the luncheon and heard Dick Williams introduce the entire Red Sox squad, and outline his plans for the 1967 season.

The BoSox Club, for years, has been what Coleman was able to describe as "the most successful club in the country." Around the turn of the century, there were close to 900 members. To become a member, one had to be sponsored by another member. (This was not a rigorous process, but this author of this brief history of the club is pleased to have been sponsored by Lib Dooley.) It's easier to become a member these days. One can simply go to the www.bosoxclub.org site and find your way to the membership section.

The Club meets monthly throughout the baseball season, with guests from the Red Sox and the visiting club in town at the time of any given luncheon. The luncheons averaged around 325 members, though the November 2007 luncheon drew well over 500. The Club also organizes spring training junkets and its 2006 banquet in Fort Myers fed 200 members. The BoSox Club gives out a number of scholarships to baseball camps and other honors to school ballplayers, and organizes an annual spring training jaunt as well. When the Red Sox are in need of additional volunteers to help staff certain events, they will often reach out to the ranks of the BoSox Club as well. Among Red Sox team personnel, Dick Bresciani had been the valued long-time liaison to the BoSox Club. Pam Kenn of the Red Sox has now assumed the role of liaison and serves on the club's board of directors.

We will return to a more detailed look at the BoSox Club after considering two other groups, one a little older, and one which is younger.

The BLOHARDS

BLOHARDS stands for the Benevolent Loyal Order of Honorable Ancient Red Sox Diehard Sufferers. This fan club holds luncheon meetings twice a year in the heart of the beast—New York City—at the time of a Red Sox series with their rivals in the Bronx. For good measure, the Club also hosts an annual bus trip to the home opener at Fenway Park, several viewing parties at various watering holes over the course of the season and, when feeling particularly ambitious, a field trip to see the Olde Towne Team in action at either Yankee Stadium or Citi Field.

The group is said to have been formed in 1964 in a New Haven Railroad bar car after a Sox-Yanks confrontation at the Stadium, when Henry Berry happened upon Jim Powers as Powers sang: "Who's better than his brother Joe? Dominic DiMaggio…"[59] They swapped stories and, Berry wrote, "By the time the train reached Darien I was not only a member of the Club but its Vice President-Historian."[60]

In the days prior to the three World Series championships, the mood of the luncheons was what George Kimball once called "approximately three hours of self-flagellation."[61] Early meetings were held at Danny's Hideaway, a chic steakhouse/nightclub, and were frequently attended by the then-serving Red Sox managers, including Johnny Pesky and Eddie Kasko. Subsequent gatherings were held at the Hotel Lexington, the McGraw-Hill Dining Room and, at a low ebb in the team's and the Club's fortunes, among the mounted moose heads in the canteen room of the Park Avenue Armory, where guests would occasionally share the single cramped elevator with residents of the co-located homeless shelter.

The Club has historically taken pride in keeping its cost of participation as low as possible. The price of a BLOHARDS luncheon in 1969 was $5.00, the same price as the Club's annual dues in 1979. Buoyed by a flattering piece in the *New York Post* the paid membership rolls swelled to about 350 by mid-1983, propelling the Club to its heyday of A-list luncheon guests and sold-out luncheons. Over thirty years later the 2017 annual membership charge will be just $20.00, with younger/healthier members invited to purchase lifetime memberships at $150.00 "cheap."

Today, the Club's venue of choice is the prestigious Yale Club where, during propitious times, crowds of 200 or more have again come out for the luncheons. And it was the Yale Club where the 2004 World Championship Trophy made one of its first public appearances during a specially-convened celebration of over 350 BLOHARDS to mark the occasion of the long-awaited Holy Grail. Obviously lacking for both celebrities and sober non-celebrities, MLB Radio's (and WFAN's) Ed Randall famously conducted a 20-minute in-depth live on-air interview with the World Series Trophy, channeled on that evening by BLOHARDS' Assistant to the Summer Intern to the Traveling Secretary, Joe Cosgriff.

As with several other organization luminaries, Jim Powers and Henry Berry enjoyed professional careers in publishing and advertising. Powers, who served as President of the BLOHARDS until his death in 2005, was the publisher of *Parade* Magazine and *USA Weekend* (and a native of Uxbridge, Massachusetts), while Hartford native Berry, who once served as the international advertising manager for *Business Week*, served as the Club's V.P. and Historian.[62] In this latter capacity, Berry's entertaining presentations at BLOHARDS lunches came to feature both examples from his extensive baseball card collection and the highly-anticipated "Horse's Ass" Award. As with so many loyal Sox fans of post-World War I vintage, Berry died without having seen the Red Sox win a World Series championship. His legacy carries on, however, with the "Henry Berry Memorial Slideshow," narrated by Southie native Ray Duffy, with Alex Rodriguez having joined George Steinbrenner as a "Lifetime Achievement Recipient" of the HAA.

Among the celebrities who've been members of the club are Cleveland Amory, Joseph Abboud, and Yale President A. Bartlett Giamatti, who wrote back after receiving solicitation to join, (and with his tongue clearly in his cheek) enthused that the Club's invitation was "the biggest thing that ever happened to him."[63] Other notables have included film critic Jeffery Lyons and jazz singer/guitarist John Pizzarelli, who has entertained luncheons with such Sox-themed ditties as "My Bobby Valentine," "Jacoby Ellsbury (to the tune of "Hooray for Hollywood"), and "Jenks for the Memories." At some point during the turbulent early 1980's then-Broadway singer and current Yankee broadcaster Suzyn Waldman saw her request to become a Club executive denied by a controversial 3-2 vote at a time when that "honor" was reserved only for males.

Red Sox fans who pre-date the three world championships won in the early 21st century will recognize Amory's sentiments when he said, "We are New England Puritans who are not allowed to be happy. We all suffer from a beautiful form of masochism. I have a feeling that deep down inside we all have a death wish; otherwise we wouldn't be Red Sox fans. Do you know what it's like to have been a Red Sox fan living in New York for 30 years?"[64] In 1991, film critic Jeffrey Lyons said, "The last time the Red Sox won a World Series....there was a Russian revolution."[65] Jim Powers added, "There's a saying in Boston: 'They did it to our fathers, they're doing it to us.'"[66] Without denying this fatalism, the BLOHARDS always leavened it with humor and a stubborn insistence that better days were ahead, as, in fact, they were. (See 2004, 2007, 2013.)

The early days of the BLOHARDS were frequently characterized by off-center behavior and a distinguished cast of characters. The *Boston Herald* once called them a "slightly daffy collection of relocated Red Sox rooters."[67] And while John Lacy of the *Hartford Courant* wrote of Henry Berry, "He appears perfectly normal,"[68] there seemed to be at least as much evidence on the opposite side of that argument. In fact, a source quoted in Lacy's story more accurately referred to Berry as "one of the nuttiest Red Sox fans in Connecticut," a role Henry played with gusto during his professional commuting via Metro North and its predecessors.

It was in 1968 that Berry came up with the idea of chartering buses to transport BLOHARDS to Opening Day at Fenway Park and, for the most part, home again. By 1979, these pilgrimages became so popular that Berry mandated that reservations needed to be made in January. For quite a while, ridership reflected an earlier tradition and the thinking of a bygone era. As late as 1983, even when Berry estimated that the club was about 50% women, he decreed, "Only men are allowed on the bus to Fenway. We've got to draw the line somewhere."[69] Today, the Opening Day trip is run by Berry's designated successor Ray Duffy and has grown to two full buses, one of which is principally ridden by female BLOHARDS.

The Red Sox organization has always favored the BLOHARDS. "We recognize they are in the belly of the beast and we try to give them as much moral support as possible," says Boston's fiery former-president, Larry Lucchino, a favorite of the BLOHARDS. "We appreciate their support as well as their courage."[70] Other members of the Sox hierarchy who've been especially supportive of the group include longtime Red Sox historian Dick Bresciani, current team historian Gordon Edes, Community Relations Manager Sarah Narracci, and former Sox EVP Dr. Charles Steinberg.

Addressing the succession of pioneering co-founders Berry and Powers, the BLOHARDS installed a Board of six that runs the organization today: Julie Killian and Sarah Powers (both daughters of Jim Powers), Jim Shea, Ray Duffy, Joe Cosgriff, and Peter Collery. Like the BoSox Club, a membership organization, one suspects that collection of dues is not the highest of priorities—witness Jim Shea's response when asked how many members the organization had at the start of 2007: "I'm guessing that there are around 800 on the e-mail list, but I don't know how many are paid up."

Groucho Marx said he'd never want to join a club that would have him for a member. We're not sure what that has to do with anything here, but this is a club which includes among its key events a 1992 fiasco that reads thusly: "Butch Hobson, newly-appointed as manager of the Red Sox, essentially challenges a by-now age-enfeebled Henry Berry to a fist fight during an early April BLOHARDS confab at the McGraw-Hill building. Berry's crime? Gentle mockery of Hobson's mentor and the team's new third base coach, Don Zimmer. In three subsequent seasons as Sox skipper, Hobson fails to ever bring the team in above .500." The event also confirmed the Board's suspicions going in—that a happy-hour start time, an outspoken membership, a fiery new manager, and an open bar had the potential to produce fireworks.

The assembled sufferers were kinder to Jimy Williams, about whom they graciously comment: "Immensely likeable, during a 45-minute conversation in which he never once gives a straightforward answer to any remotely controversial question." Starting with Kasko and Pesky, from Williams, Dick to Williams, Jimy, virtually every Sox manager (except Kevin Kennedy) appeared before the BLOHARDS. Of Dan Duquette, the website chronology notes: "Notwithstanding his reputation, he is gracious, relaxed and funny."

Notwithstanding the perception that players' arms were twisted and then twisted again before they would "agree" to attend BLOHARDS' luncheons, there are more than a few indications that the Club's guests took their duties seriously. In the *2007 Boston Red Sox Media Guide*, among the personal information listed for pitcher Javier Lopez—along with the name of his high school, his college baseball statistics, that he was Colorado's player rep for a year, and his marriage to Renee....was the unmistakable pinnacle of his lifetime accomplishments: "Attended luncheons in 2006 for the BoSox Club and the BLOHARDS."

In a nod to the Club's "graying" demographic, the BLOHARDS described themselves in a press release as a social service organization that provides a hot lunch program to senior citizens. They also provided referrals to Sox-friendly bars and other "safe spaces" in New York as well as information about field trips to Fenway for deprived tri-state area residents. While this description of the Club was likely made in jest, there is often much truth in humor. For more than fifty years the BLOHARDS have truly provided strength and succor to one of the most oppressed minorities in New York—Red Sox fans living behind enemy lines. Considering its continuing vibrancy, the Club seems set to do so for years to come.

Are you in the city, with time on your hands? These days, there are not just one, or two, but five bars in New York City which cater to Red Sox fans, all promoted on the www.blohards.com website: Professor Thom's, The Hairy Monk, Pat O'Brien's Bar, Standings Bar, and The Riviera Café.

Two BLOHARDS bus groups – the first bus in 1967, and a recent bus in 2011. Photographs courtesy of Peter M. Collery and Joseph Cosgriff.

Bluenose Bosox Brotherhood

The Bluenose Bosox Brotherhood is proof positive that Red Sox Nation has no borders. The BBB is a diehard group of Sox fans from Nova Scotia, "Bluenose" being a nickname for residents of that Canadian province. Launched in 2005 by Annapolis Valley residents Don Hyslop, Dave Ritcey, and Jim Prime, the Bluenose Bosox Brotherhood has grown to approximately 100 members from across the province. The club has become so popular that plans are underway to create BBB chapters in various parts of the province.

Bill "Spaceman" Lee is the BBB's "Emperor for Life," Johnny Pesky is the "Patron Saint," and Dick Gernert is "Ambassador-at-Large."

One BBB coup was convincing the Red Sox to bring the 2007 World Series trophy to Halifax, the capital city, in January of 2008. The connections between Boston and Halifax are many and varied. In 1917, when the Halifax Explosion devastated the city and left thousands dead and wounded, it was Boston that came to its aid most quickly and effectively. Nova Scotians have never forgotten that act of compassion and every year a Christmas tree arrives in the Massachusetts capital as a token of gratitude. There are numerous historical, cultural, business, and family ties between Nova Scotia and Massachusetts. One of the most enduring is a mutual love of the Red Sox. Prior to the existence of the Montreal Expos in 1969 and the Toronto Blue Jays in 1977, the Red Sox were the "home team" for most Nova Scotia baseball fans. Countless fans of an earlier generation huddled around their radios to pick up scratchy broadcasts of Sox games. Today many people make the annual trip to Fenway Park to see their favorites in action. Countless others have invested in satellite dishes so that they don't miss a game.

The BBB meets on a semi-regular basis to discuss all things Red Sox. There are plans to make road trips to Boston as well as Pawtucket,

Lowell, and Portland, Maine. Funds made from auctions and other activities are donated to children's charities such as the Jimmy Fund, the IWK Children's Hospital, and minor league baseball. As the book goes to press, we hear word of a possible Herring Choker branch in neighboring New Brunswick, perhaps to be organized by Bruce MacDonald from Ted Williams' old stomping grounds on the Miramichi River.

BBB insignia and t-shirt images, courtesy of Jim Prime.

The BoSox Club

The BoSox Club was born on February 15, 1967 at Fenway Park and "a meeting of 50 prominent Boston businessmen elected former Hose outfielder Dom DiMaggio president."[71] The *Globe*'s Harold Kaese immediately put the new club in perspective, naming the Royal Rooters. Kaese quoted (in full?) DiMaggio's "somewhat terse message in his inaugural address."[72] DiMaggio said, "Our goal is to help the club, the players and baseball in any way we can." Answering some questions, he said that they had not decided on membership yet, but had sent out 80 letters and had 80 positive responses. He added, "We want players to meet people in the business community. We'd like a closer relationship. It will mean more opportunities off the field for the players." These were still the days when players almost invariably needed

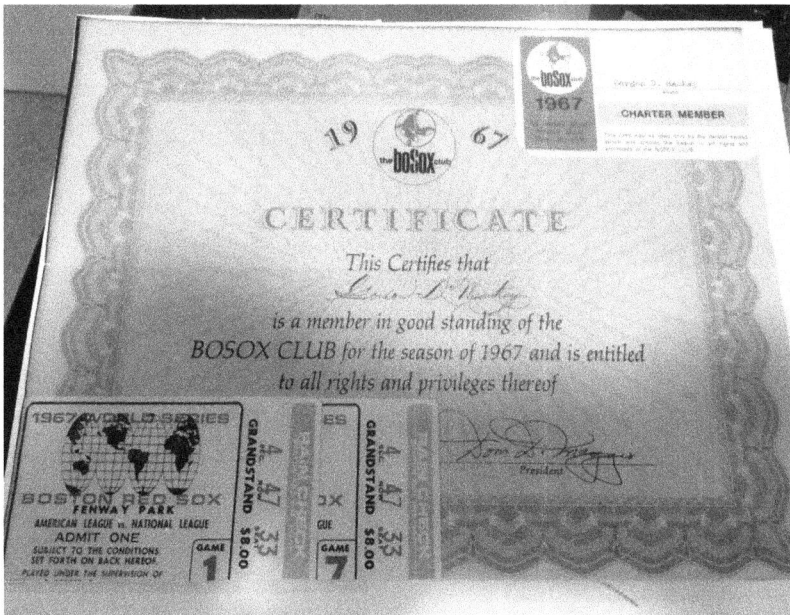

Gordon MacKay's membership certificate, and World Series tickets, 1967.

offseason work to supplement their salaries. The team's biggest star, Carl Yastrzemski, had just had his salary increased to $50,000 in 1966.

There was, from the start, a commitment to a degree of community service. DiMaggio said, "We plan to recognize and honor high school, college, Little League, sandlot players and teams. We'll probably give some award to Red Sox players at the end of the season. We're hoping to have a lot of fun."[73]

Kaese said that the club was indeed modeled on Cleveland's Wahoo Club and that Ken Coleman had been instrumental in the formation of the BoSox Club. He told of Al Rosen's phoning to the meeting.

He also noted that the Patriots "have the backing of a similar organization—the 1776 Club."

The club planned to hold 11 or 12 luncheons throughout the season, and named some of the organizers, those who, in addition to Dom DiMaggio, became the initial officers: Bradford C. Jernegan, Vice President; Larry Polans, Vice President; Edward Hanify and Truman Casner, Legal Advisors. Directors of the club included Bernard Baldwin, Dean M. Boylan, Thomas J. Feenan, Robert Cheyne, Clarence E. March, and James Kelso. The *Record American* and the *Traveler* both listed the business affiliations of each of the club's directors.[74]

The first luncheon was held at Anthony's Pier Four on April 10, to welcome the team back from spring training.

The First Luncheon

Dick Williams enthused about the 1967 Red Sox at that first April 10 BoSox Club luncheon. Though Clif Keane of the *Globe* noted that "he had barked at them all spring," in front of the "250 Boston businessmen" (the *Record American* said 350) assembled for the luncheon, he "praised his guys so hard a few of them must have wondered if he meant them, really." Williams, noted for believing he had to ride George Scott to get the most out of him, said, "George Scott has the magic touch with the glove. He could be one of the great ones. I

First road trip, August 28, 1967 flight to New York. Dave Morehead shut out the Yankees, 3-0.

look for him to do great things. Stand up, George."[75] Williams then introduced each member of the team, saying something positive about each one. He said, "Our outfield is the best in the league" and said as long as he was with the team, he would never let Yaz go. He called Tony Conigliaro "the best right fielder in the American League" and said, "There's no telling what his potential is."

Dick O'Connell talked at the luncheon, too, and said, "In all my years with the Red Sox, I have never seen a team in such good condition."

DiMaggio said they had received over 1,000 applications for membership but had been forced to limit it initially, though they hoped to gradually increase it in time.

A second luncheon was held on May 19 at the Hotel Somerset. Cleveland GM Gabe Paul spoke, saying that baseball would never ask for special exemptions for players subject to the call for military service. He declared that Dick Williams' 1967 Red Sox were the most improved team in the league. Other speakers included Indians manager Joe Adcock, sportscaster Bob Neal, pitchers Sam McDowell and Steve Hargan, BoSox president DiMaggio, Red Sox broadcaster Ken Coleman, and first baseman George Scott.

Just four days after Tony Conigliaro's serious beaning, the Club held another luncheon at the Somerset. Speakers included Ken McMullen and Bob Priddy of the Washington Senators, both of whom predicted the Red Sox would win the pennant.[76]

On August 28, some 79 members of the club (and Massachusetts Gov. John Volpe) flew on American Airlines to New York and then took a chartered bus to Yankee Stadium for "Carl Yastrzemski Night" ceremonies. Prices were more modest at the time — $26.25 covered roundtrip bus and airfare, and a ticket to the game.[77] State treasurer Robert Crane, legal counsel Joseph Tauro, and four other state officials were part of the party. Carl Yastrzemski, "the man they call Yaz," accepted a few gifts but had asked for most gifts to be in the form of donations to the Jimmy Fund, Boston's landmark charity organized to fight cancer in children. The Jimmy Fund netted around $10,000. [78]

The Club was disappointed on September 1 when Eddie Stanky bowed out of that day's luncheon, purportedly due to a "previous commitment" but — guessed the *Cleveland Plain Dealer*'s Russell Schneider — perhaps because he didn't want to get into a public war of words with Boston's acerbic Clif Keane, who had written an article critical of Stanky's White Sox in a recent *Sports Illustrated.* Schneider noted that the BoSox Club was "the equivalent of Cleveland's Wahoo Club."[79] Ken Coleman was the emcee. Both Ken Boyer and Pete Ward of the White Sox did come to the luncheon, as did Red Sox personnel director Haywood Sullivan and recently-acquired Red Sox outfielder Ken Harrelson (who talked mostly about golf.)[80]

There was another luncheon just two weeks later, on September 15. The Baltimore Orioles were in town and both All-Star third baseman Brooks Robinson and manager Hank Bauer came to the event, Bauer posing for some photographs arm-wrestling with Dick Williams. For the Red Sox, Elston Howard (another midseason acquisition) also appeared.

On Friday, September 29, just as the team entered its dramatic final weekend series against the Minnesota Twins, the BoSox Club held its third luncheon of the month, with Ken Coleman as toastmaster. Rico Petrocelli was given an award, intended to become annual, as the most underrated Red Sox player of the year. Yaz had been the only Sox player to know in advance that the award was to be presented to Rico, and requested to be the one to present it, but that morning he had to rush home to his son Mike, who had been hospitalized for appendicitis the night before. There was no operation and Mike returned home on Friday morning. All this was on Yaz's mind as he went on a 10-for-14 tear with nine RBIs over the final four games, Thursday through Sunday. The award to Rico was presented by Red Sox veteran infielder Ted Lepcio.

Dick Williams received a community service award in the form of an admiral's chair. All the Red Sox players and coaches were in attendance, and Williams introduced them.

Other awards were given to coach Art Kersey and team captain Dave Polcari for bringing Medford High the Eastern Massachusetts Class A title. Coach (and former Sox player) Eddie Pellagrini of Boston College was honored for helping B.C. become the top team in New England, and manager Joe Cunningham and team owner Frank Passanesi of the Boston Park League champion Supreme Saluts were honored as well.[81]

At year's end, the club had held 12 luncheons, one with each visiting team, and had 320 members who had paid $10.00 apiece before new applications were cut off in August. DiMaggio said they planned to reopen it with a next goal of 500. "The problem," he said, "is getting places large enough to hold the luncheons. That's quite a crowd, 500."[82] In the same summary article, Clif Keane said that the club was contemplating a trip to Winter Haven from March 9-14, 1968. Some 45 members had raised their hands at the final luncheon of the season, indicating their interest to take a five-day trip to spring training. Keane said Winter Haven was the kind of place where you could "go out on the town and be back in 10 minutes" and where "eating oranges around the pool is the wildest of parties for nightlifers." He figured if the BoSox Club descended on the place, the natives might be talking about it for the next 50 years.

The First Spring Training Trip and the Second Season

The first person to sign up for the spring training trip was, as it happens, Ted Lepcio.[83] The package cost $189, which included four exhibition games and five nights at the new Sheraton Hotel in Cypress Gardens, "an organized safari to a training camp."[84] The trip was organized by Garden City Tours and was booked to capacity, the total party numbering 114.

The club met on February 7 at the Somerset and expanded to 10 members, adding Lepcio and Eddie Pellagrini, Dick Casey, and Harry Carlson to the board of directors. Dom DiMaggio was reelected as president, Jernegan as VP and treasurer, Paul Murphy was made secretary, and Truman Casner the legal adviser. Ken Coleman was an honorary member of the board. They announced an April 15 "Welcome Home" dinner for the Red Sox, the day before the home opener.[85]

They met again on June 5, with Denny McLain among the guests. The club announced a contest asking boys in two age groups (12-14, and 15-16) to write in 250 words or less why they would like to be selected to be able to spend a week from August 25-31 at the Ted Williams baseball camp in Lakeville, Massachusetts, with the BoSox Club sponsoring the contest to select 15 boys.[86]

Lefty Gomez attended the June 28 luncheon at the Somerset. Eddie Popowski was there, too. On August 1, Ken Harrelson was the guest, appearing in powder blue Nehru jacket and slacks, with a white turtleneck and a gold medallion with five colored stones.[87] On August 16, some 600 members (with wives and children) attended an evening dinner at the Statler Hilton. Dick Williams came, as did the players and coaches, and the front office. On August 28, the club held its first Family Night at Fenway Park. At the final 1968 luncheon on September 27, Mike Andrews was unanimously acclaimed as Red Sox Player of the Year.[88] Awards were given to former FBI agent Chuck Toomey of the Red Sox front office as "humanitarian of the year," to the Harvard baseball team, to the West Roxbury Little League champs, and to the Bob Woolf Club of the Boston Park League. Ken Coleman was the emcee.

Closing Out the 1960s and Into the 1970s

At its first meeting of 1969, in early January, club members had an advance screening of the 1968 World Series film showing the Tigers beating the Cardinals, the first promotional film made by Major League Baseball Promotion Corp.

In January 1969, Brad Jernegan (treasurer of State Street Bank and Trust) was voted the second president of the BoSox Club. Dom DiMaggio remained on the board. Ted Lepcio became vice president, with James Kelso as treasurer and Harry E. Carlson as secretary. The board of directors was joined by Dean Boylan, Ken Coleman, Dick Donovan, and Eddie Pellagrini.

There was a "welcome home" dinner with the entire ballclub on April 17. The first luncheon of the season, also at the Somerset, was held on May 21 with Dick Williams, George Thomas, and Joe Azcue, with Bill Rigney, Rick Reichardt, and Dick Stuart of the California Angels, and their announcer Dick Enberg. On June 2 the lineup was Dick Williams, Ray Culp, and Garry Roggenburk for the Red Sox, and Tommy John and Bill Melton of the White Sox along with their manager Don Gutteridge and GM Ed Short.

The "Why I Would Like To Spend A Week at Ted Williams' Camp" letter-writing competition was again offered to boys who were members of Little League, Babe Ruth, etc. baseball teams in the region.

Billy Martin spoke at the monthly luncheon on August 19. Halsey Hall, Twins broadcaster, introduced Martin. The 15 winners of the Ted Williams Camp award were introduced. The Red Sox were represented by Mike Andrews and Mike Nagy.

The club held a "cookout" at Fenway Park on August 26. There was a luncheon on September 2, when Kansas City was in town, and another one on September 18 which featured Earl Weaver and Mark

A very early board of directors photograph, ca. 1968. Back row, L to R: unknown, Thomas Feenan, Clarence March, Ted Lepcio, Harry Carlson, Bob Cheyne. Front row, L to R: Truman Casner, Larry Polans, Pres. Dom DiMaggio, Brad Jernegan, Ken Coleman.

Belanger of the Orioles, and coach Darrell Johnson and Carlton Fisk for the Red Sox. Lee Stange was selected as Man of the Year, the honor presented at the final luncheon on September 26. UMass was given the college award, and Newton High the high school award. The Craven club was the winner of the Boston Park League. Tom Dowd was the principal speaker. Red Sox publicity director Bill Crowley presented a special award to Dick Casey, who had been associated with baseball in the Boston area all the way back to 1912. About 200 attended.

Another spring training tour was organized in 1970; it was a seven-day package costing $206; some 102 club members joined the tour. The club had hosted the first public showing of the 1969 World Series film at their January 22 luncheon. All of the 1969 officers were re-elected in January 1970. The board also comprised Dean Boylan (Boston Sand and Gravel), Robert Cheyne (VP of the *Boston Herald Traveler*), Dick Casey, honorary member Ken Coleman, Dom DiMaggio, Dick Donovan, Tom Feenan, Tom Kinnealey, Clarence March, Leonard "Lefty" Nelson of Wilson Sporting Goods, and Eddie Pellagrini. Three Red Sox pitchers — Sparky Lyle, Dick Mills, and Eddie Phillips held a brief interview session, a panel.

The Red Sox were honored at a 1970 Welcome Home dinner held at the Statler on April 22. The first luncheon during the season was on May 19 with Eddie Kasko, Gary Peters, and Luis Alvarado. Mike Kilkenny and Cesar Gutierrez represented the Tigers. The June 19 luncheon featured Ralph Houk, Phil Rizzuto, Bob Gamere, and Yankees PR man Bob Fishel. The Red Sox were represented by Haywood Sullivan, George Thomas, and Sparky Lyle, with former player and Red Sox scout Jumpin' Joe Dugan.

The Ted Williams Camp sponsorship continued. The August 16, 1970 *Herald* ran a photograph of that year's winners.

On July 20, Dom DiMaggio introduced a resolution, which the BoSox Club unanimously adopted, calling for interleague play. Fans, the resolution said, should be given "the privilege of seeing the outstanding players of each league play." It was addressed to Commissioner Bowie Kuhn and the presidents of the National and American leagues, and officials of the various ballclubs.[89] This was somewhat represented by articles such as one which ran in the *Los Angeles Times* which mentioned DiMaggio as a director of the BoSox Club, "whose chief aim is to help inaugurate inter-league play in the majors."[90]

In November 1970, the club was reported to number 550. At the annual meeting, held at the Sheraton Plaza, Ted Lepcio was elected president and Dick Donovan as vice president.[91]

The first charter member the club lost was sportswriter and publicist Joseph McKenney, age 51, who died of a massive coronary on July 21, 1970. He had been former publicity director of the American League.

In January 1971, *Herald* reporter Tim Horgan interviewed Dom DiMaggio about a number of subjects. DiMaggio said, "Baseball can't seem to understand that the good old days are going. The game doesn't have the field to itself any longer. It has to compete for attention with so many other sports. But it doesn't." He cited a BoSox Club luncheon as one illustration. "During the season we hold luncheons and invite players from the visiting teams to attend. One day last summer, we invited the Yankees, but nobody showed. We found out later the players were told they didn't have to come. So naturally they didn't." He added, "One reason I liked Dick Williams when he managed the Sox was because he went everywhere to promote the game. He never passed up a speaking engagement. He talked to the fans, so his players did, too."[92]

The BoSox Club itself sold out its now-annual spring training trip again. About 130 comprised the 1971 contingent. An overflow crowd packed out Anthony's Pier 4 for the homecoming luncheon on April 22, with Eddie Kasko. The second luncheon, on April 30, featured Harvey Haddix, Ken Tatum, and Duane Josephson, and Bert Blyleven, Bill Rigney, and Dan Thompson of the Twins. The May 28 luncheon drew over 300 people who welcomed Oakland A's manager Dick Williams back to Boston. Catfish Hunter and Dick Green came

As was often the case back in the day, many events were almost exclusively male, as indicated in this club photograph at a downtown Boston location in the early 1970s.

from the A's, while the Red Sox were represented by Bill Lee and Sparky Lyle and Eddie Popowski.

The luncheons had now moved to Anthony's Pier 4, where they would be for more or less the next quarter century.[93] The noontime June 21 luncheon included a special presentation to Will "Cannonball" Jackman, described by many as one of the greatest pitchers of all time—compared to Waller Johnson and to Satchel Paige. Like Paige, Jackman—who lived in Massachusetts from 1924 to his death in 1972—was confined to pitching in the Negro Leagues, and for teams such as the Boston Colored Giants in the Greater Boston Colored League.[94]

The August 17 Family Night at Fenway attracted over 1,000 members and family. On December 17, BoSox Club co-founder Brad Jernegan died, at age 59. More than 40 years later, the club still awards an annual Brad Jernegan Award. Recipients are noted at the end of this volume.

Many of the activities, of course, became annual events—the spring training trip (140, in 1972), etc. etc. Lee Cummings of Dorchester and John Hurley, a clerk of courts in Boston, joined the board in April 1972. Guests that year included Earl Weaver, Merv Rettenmund, Don Baylor, Eddie Kasko, "Super Sub" John Kennedy, Bill Freehan, Charlie Silvera, Eddie Brinkman, Don Newhauser, and Bob Montgomery.

Come 1973, the local press called the BoSox Club the most successful such club of its sort in the major leagues. "It was patterned on the Wahoo Club in Cleveland and has surpassed it," said Red Sox PR director Bill Crowley. Atlanta has a similar program that has met with very good success but none has enjoyed the reception the BoSox Club has experienced." President Bob Cheyne said, "We've always enjoyed the cooperation of the visiting teams. The managers, the broadcasters and the top players are willing to attend and take part. And it's true of all the clubs. Many of the visiting managers tell us they wish they had something like it."[95] Membership was still $10 at the time, plus the cost of attending the luncheons.

Carlton Fisk and other Sox players sign autographs for BoSox Club members and families at Fenway event.

Umpire Nestor Chylak was a hit at the June 26, 1973 luncheon, which drew 337 attendees. Tommy Harper received the Man of the Year award in September.

In 1974, there were 130 on the spring training trip. The club's Bob Cheyne helped Eddie Pellagrini set up a month-long series of baseball clinics at various locations in Eastern Massachusetts, for both boys and girls, which was sponsored by Coca-Cola and WHDH.[96] Cheyne was in the news again when he won a trip to Spain, a prize donated to a raffle that was part of the Jimmy Fund golf tournament at the Colonial Country Club. For whatever reasons, the club began to get less ink as the years rolled by.

Carl Yastrzemski was the main speaker at the September 1975 luncheon.

A total of 194 took the spring training trip in 1976, perhaps energized by the Red Sox winning the American League pennant in 1975.

The number totaled over 200 later in the 1970s, and in the waning years of the decade there was formed, locally, a BoSox Club of Winter Haven.[97]

They invited Boston Celtics coach Red Auerbach to the first luncheon in 1976. All the new players on the team, except that night's stating pitcher Ferguson Jenkins, came to the first luncheon as well. For the annual BoSox Club Family Day kids outing in August 1976, 23 members of the team including manager Don Zimmer came to the event.[98]

The scholarships to the Ted Williams Camp completed its 10th year. There were between 1,000 and 1,500 entries each year, reported club president Clarence March in April 1978, and 10 members of the BoSox Club read through each one to select the 15 winning entries. The dues in 1978 were $20 and the cost of the luncheons had also increased, to $7.50. March said the club numbered 500 and had a lengthy waiting list, governed by the capacity of the Pier 4 dining area.[99]

Occasionally, there was some controversy. At the May 9, 1978 luncheon, it was reported that Don Zimmer "didn't pull any punches…[he] lashed out at Rick Wise, Ferguson Jenkins, and Jim Willoughby."[100] He actually was praising the 1978 Red Sox, in the process indicating that the 1977 club had had some complainers on the team. Jenkins had been a favorite among club members when he was with the Texas Rangers, arrived at Boston at 7 AM after a lengthy six-hour team flight delay, but still came to the noon luncheon.[101] George Scott, though, was a no-show for the May 31, 1977 luncheon prompting a quip about it being the first meal he'd missed all season.[102]

Anthony Anathas (of Pier 4) knocked down an interior wall to create more space, after five overflow luncheons in a row, and the August 2, 1978 luncheon drew a record 540 attendees.

Many of those who were members at the time appear to have taken membership as a point of some distinction, one may conclude by seeing the number of people whose obituaries indicated that the BoSox Club was one of the organizations to which the recently-deceased person had belonged. By the later 1980s, the number of obituaries containing references to the club increased as the founding or early members of the club began to die with more frequency.

When Tom Yawkey was inducted at Cooperstown, some 80 members of the BoSox Club (as well as the entire front office of the team) were present.

The 1980s

On November 20, 1981, when Red Sox PR man Bill Crowley retired, there was a retirement event for him at Pier 4, sponsored by the BoSox Club and drawing 200, including Commissioner Bowie Kuhn and—both impressively and touchingly—some 24 Fenway Park ushers.[103]

For whatever reason, Yankees owners George Steinbrenner was reported by Peter Gammons in June 1982 to have "1. refused to allow his players to attend the Bosox Club Luncheon and 2. had ordered his PR people to say he wasn't at the game."[104]

The following month, the Club showed again its commitment to diversity of a different sort inviting longtime member of the Fenway Park ground crew Al Forester to talk to its July 27 luncheon. Forester is, to some, best known as the employee who drove the golf cart in which Ted Williams was seated to the ceremony at the pitcher's mound at the 1999 All-Star Game at Fenway Park.

On September 30, 1983, two days before his final retirement day, Carl Yastrzemski was again the speaker at a BoSox Club luncheon. He wrote a column which ran in the *Herald* in which he said, "Yesterday at the BoSox Club luncheon, I received its annual Man of the Year award. I appreciated it very much because the BoSox Club has been one of the greatest supporters of the Red Sox over the years and also of organized baseball in Massachusetts and New England."[105] It was part of a very busy time, so busy he forgot to eat, he told Leigh Montville of the *Globe*. After the BoSox Club event, he went to a downtown hotel to greet arriving friends and relatives. He didn't get to bed until 2, but was unable to sleep. "Why am I so hungry"? he asked himself. "I am hungry," he finally decided, "because I haven't eaten all day. I forgot to eat."[106]

In 1984, the club launched a $25 for 25 campaign to raise money for Tony Conigliaro, who had suffered a heart attack and irreversible brain damage in early 1982. Donors received a Tony C model

Louisville Slugger. The rest of the money went towards Tony's care. By May, over 500 bats had been ordered. The club's first luncheon, in April, was to feature Ralph Houk, Oil Can Boyd, Mike Easler, Jackie Gutierrez, and Al Nipper.

Mike Easler was a guest of the club at Winter Haven; in the September, he was named Man of the Year. The BoSox Club and the Boston Park league co-hosted a May dinner in Randolph, honoring co-founder (and former Fenway Park usher) Dick Casey's 90th birthday, with proceeds going to the Jimmy Fund. Haywood Sullivan attended the September luncheon — and handed retiring Red Sox manager Ralph Houk the keys to a Cadillac Seville. Easler and Sox owner Jean Yawkey were also both honored at the September event.

It was at a 1984 luncheon that Chuck Waseleski, "The Maniacal One," began to earn broader recognition for his idiosyncratic compilations of statistical oddities. He had gone to the luncheon and met both Peter Gammons and Joe Castiglione. "They talked statistics and soon the Waseleski report was going to them as well as to Bill James."[107]

Al Nipper and Glenn Hoffman talked at a July 1985 luncheon about how they conspired with Marty Barrett and executed a hidden ball trick on Doug DeCinces of the Angels.

The club continued to sponsor campers during the summer. The July 1986 luncheon was scheduled to present an unusual duo — Oil Can Boyd and Rey Quinones. And George Steinbrenner's ban was still in effect, wrote Dan Shaughnessy: "Yankees owner George Steinbrenner has ruled that his players may not attend distractive functions such as the BoSox Club luncheon that was held Tuesday when the Yanks were in town. Coach Roy White represented the Pinstripe Gang."[108] This was, however, the year that Boyd "stormed out of Fenway Park" when he learned that he had not been selected to take part in the 1986 All-Star Game. He was suspended without pay for a minimum of three days, and prohibited from returning at all until he apologized to his teammates, said GM Lou Gorman. Larry Whiteside wrote in the July 12 *Boston Globe*: "Boyd failed to appear

1985 - 86
report

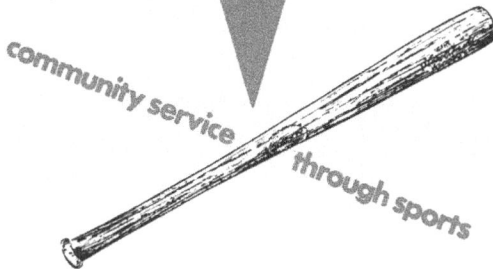

the **boSox** club

community service

through sports

Printed 1985–86 report.

for last night's game and also missed an appearance before the BoSox Club yesterday afternoon."[109]

A special luncheon in January 1987 celebrated the 20th anniversary of the BoSox Club. In May, Roger Clemens wrote a lengthy article for the *Boston Herald,* in which he mentioned the club. In part, he wrote, "I enjoy the fans. I don't care what any ballplayer says: when you work hard at something and hear all that applause rain down on you when you've done a good job, it's the greatest feeling in the world. I enjoy getting to meet people in person, so they have an idea what we're like as people as well as ballplayers. I enjoy things like the BoSox club luncheons. I enjoy going to hospitals and meeting the kids."[110]

Occasionally a controversy might break out from something that was said at a BoSox Club gathering. "Reliever Joe Sambito has issued an apology to the bleacher fans in Section 34," wrote Larry Whiteside in early July 1987, "where his stock dropped dramatically after some off-the-cuff remarks recently at a BoSox Club luncheon. The remarks questioned the IQ of bleacher fans, and have been widely circulated. 'I guess what I said was too general,' said Sambito. 'There are many loyal fans out there, especially in Section 34.'"[111]

More than 1,600 turned out for Family Day in 1987 (it was seen as "Autograph Day" in those days, with almost every member of the team greeting the youngsters and signing autographs.) On November 20, there was a double celebration — the 20th anniversary of the Impossible Dream Red Sox and another event to celebrate the 20th anniversary of the BoSox Club, held at the Marriott at Copley Place.

In September 1988, Red Sox pitching coach Bill Fischer became the first non-player who was honored as Man of the Year by the BoSox Club, at the September 27 luncheon, recognizing his community service and contributions to the Red Sox. "Fischer coordinated youth clinics, was active in Jimmy Fund events and conducted playground group sessions as part of Mayor Flynn's drug education program."[112]

A gaffe? After the September luncheon, when the club awarded a trophy to the University of Hartford baseball team as the "college baseball team of the year," U Mass baseball coach Mike Stone "fired off a letter" to the club, complaining about "a serious injustice."[113] U Mass had been 36-16, best in New England, and voted #1 by the New England College Baseball Coaches Association. Hartford had been voted #3. In January 1989, the club presented Stone with the New England Championship trophy.

Spring 1989 saw Lou Gorman skip a BoSox Club dinner. Dan Shaughnessy reported: "Folks around the Holiday Inn pool were buzzing yesterday afternoon. Gorman was supposed to speak at a BoSox Club banquet Saturday night, but canceled because he had work to do. The affable big guy doesn't miss many meals, and veteran observers have learned that Sweet Lou's absence from the trough is usually an indication that something is in the works….Explaining his Saturday night no-show, Gorman said, "I stayed behind to do some work. The BoSox Club is tired of hearing me speak anyway. I was just working."[114]

Steve Lyons attended the April 27 luncheon — as a member of the White Sox, along with manager Jeff Torborg. Rob Murphy and Dick Berardino were there from the Red Sox. In September, Bob Stanley received a standing ovation from those assembled for the September 27; he had announced his retirement two days earlier.

1990 and the 90s

Roger Clemens was the main speaker at the April 1990 luncheon. In 1992, he received the Man of the Year award. Mentions of the club in the pages of the *Herald* more or less died out after 1991.

Given that the Red Sox were the last team in the majors to field an African American ballplayer (Pumpsie Green in 1959), journalists have always—appropriately—looked at matters of race when looking at the Red Sox.[115] In 1991, Steve Fainaru of the *Globe* noted there were two black players on the team—Ellis Burks and Mo Vaughn—and only another 13 throughout their minor-league system. Meanwhile, black fans who ventured to Fenway Park reported discouraging experiences of racism. Fainaru also observed, "The 659-member BoSox club, the largest baseball booster organization in the country, has never had a black member."[116]

Perhaps the club had not truly tired of having Lou Gorman speak; he was the main guest at the January 1993 kickoff luncheon. John Valentin and Gary Allenson spoke at the April luncheon.

In June 1994, some 60 members of the BoSox Club traveled to Cleveland to watch some Sox games. Family Day that year was canceled, however, victim to the work stoppage that saw the season end early and the absence of any World Series in 1994. Some club members did travel to Florida at spring training time 1995, but fewer than 100—more or less half of the usual 170-200.

In January 1996, GM Dan Duquette spoke at the January luncheon. A year later, at the January Pier Four luncheon, club secretary Audrey Prihoda, who had worked for the BoSox Club for 17 years, received the Brad Jernegan Award for outstanding contribution. Fan favorite, third-base coach Wendell Kim, received the Man of the Year award in September.

During spring training 1999, the highlight was when the BoSox Club members enjoyed a private luncheon with Ted Williams in

Hernando, Florida, followed by a tour of the Ted Williams Museum, located in Hernando at the time.

It was a busy year. On May 26, John Harrington hosted a reception at the World Trade Center, at which a scale model of the proposed new Fenway Park was unveiled. Club members who were present had the opportunity to meet Commissioner Bud Selig.

In July, the Red Sox hosted the All-Star Game, and the BoSox Club provided close to 300 members who assisted the Red Sox in a week of festivities up to the game itself, one notable for two things in particular. First, for the on-field arrival of Ted Williams to the delight of the crowd—and the members of baseball's "all-century team" who were on the field during pregame ceremonies. The players all flocked around Ted and would not leave, despite several admonitions from the P.A. announcer. They all wanted to be sure to say hello. When the game itself began, Pedro Martinez was the starting pitcher for the American League. The first five outs he recorded were all by way of the strikeout; Pedro won the game.

The club honored Johnny Pesky in September 1999, the year he turned 80. They thought—as did the entire baseball world—that he had been born on September 27. Only after his death did it come out that Pesky had been born on February 27.[117]

L to R: Rico Petrocelli, Bill Crowley, Johnny Pesky (Ruth Pesky in front), Walt Dropo, Mickey McDermott, Frank Malzone, 1995.

WEEI's Dave Shea with Red Sox GM Dan Duquette, 1995.

Detroit Tigers broadcaster Ernie Harwell was guest at a June 1999 luncheon.

The Year 2000 and Beyond

In early May 2000, the guest of honor was "heavy-hitting new-comer Carl Everett...feted by the BoSox Club Tuesday at Anthony's Pier 4. The 700 member-plus BoSox Club, presided over by Bill Brooks of Norwood, held a luncheon that brought 245 members into semi-intimate contact with not just Everett but veteran broadcaster Ernie Harwell, who has broadcast Tiger games since the dawn of time. Everett, in his short tenure, is on a Nomar Garciaparra-Pedro Martinez trajectory."[118] On May 25, it was Trot Nixon's turn—him and his wife Kathryn. He had thrown "caution to the wind, dove headfirst into the stands, and disappeared from view while attempting to catch a foul ball hit by the Toronto Blue Jays' Marty Cordova." He told the BoSox Club members, "'It was instinct. I'd do it all over again.' Then, he noted the 'seats were hard; they have to be 'cause they've been around since 1912.' The fans? No help at all. 'One guy was eating a hot dog and a few others were trying to get the baseball.' Second baseman Jeff Frye, who was out in the general area, yelled, 'What's the matter with you fans? Can't you at least put the ball in his glove?' Trot, by the way, isn't the only athlete in the family. His wife ran this year's Boston Marathon, collected pledges, and raised $22,000 for the Dana-Farber Cancer Institute."[119]

In 2001, Dick Flavin and the club launched an information effort to try to get Dom DiMaggio voted into the National Baseball Hall of Fame by the Veterans Committee. Unfortunately, a leading advocate—Ted Williams—was unable to pitch in, since he had underdone heart surgery in January and was recuperating. The effort fell short. In September, Ben Mondor of the Pawtucket Red Sox received the Man of the Year award, the first recipient who was neither a Red Sox player, a coach, nor a team executive.

On August 25, 2002, the Red Sox marked the 35th anniversary of the Bosox Club by honoring founder and first president, Dom DiMaggio, with a permanent plaque outside Fenway Park's Gate D, on Yawkey Way, while former BoSox Club president (and Red Sox infielder) Ted Lepcio threw out the pre-game first pitch.

In January 2004, still smarting from the Game Seven loss to the Yankees in the 2003 ALCS, the Red Sox caravan arranged for one of its stops to be at the BoSox Club luncheon in Newton. The club itself continued its annual tradition of an essay contest which would result in sending a number of youths to summer baseball camp for a week.

As hope for another run to the postseason took hold in August 2004, the *Globe*'s West edition ran a feature on the BoSox Club, which we present here in its entirety:

> Fenway Park may be the home of the Boston Red Sox, but Needham can claim to be the capital of Red Sox Nation.
>
> Out of one of the homes that line Lexington Avenue, Audrey Prihoda runs the team's official fan and booster club, the Bosox Club. Throughout the year, the club hosts a dizzying array of Red Sox-themed events including luncheons, brunches, barbecues, and awards dinners.
>
> They organize Florida road trips to spring training in Fort Myers, to minor league Sox teams in Pawtucket and Portland, Maine, and to away games.
>
> "These are diehard fans," said Prihoda, who has served as the club's executive secretary for the last 22 years. "They love the Red Sox and many are extremely opinionated. A lot are retired and they like to get together and chat" about baseball.
>
> First launched just before the 1967 "Impossible Dream" season as a way to boost sagging season ticket sales to business representatives, the club now serves to promote the Red Sox and a love of baseball at all skill levels. With close to 750 members, the club is the largest of its kind in the majors.

"They've been a strong support group ever since," said Richard Bresciani, a club board member and team liaison who is vice president for publications and archives for the Red Sox.

The club raises money for several local charities, including the Jimmy Fund and the Red Sox Foundation. Every summer, more than a dozen youngsters get scholarships to a baseball camp in Waltham run by former Sox infielder Mike Andrews.

Some of the most popular club events during the season are luncheons at the Marriott Hotel in Newton. Prihoda expects the next one, slated for Aug. 17, to draw close to 350 people.

The twice-monthly affairs feature Red Sox players, coaches, broadcasters, and management and often one or two members of whichever visiting team is in town. Except the Yankees.

"We used to invite them," said club president Cheri Giffin, known to many in Red Sox Nation as Bosox Lady. "But the Yankees would only show if they won the night before Steinbrenner would pull them [if they lost] so we dropped them."

As the club's first female president, Giffin has seen the membership expand to include a lot more women than when she first joined in 1976. "The old boy network was just raging" then. "It's quite a mix now."

With remarkable kismet, Giffin's own history as a loyal Sox fan mirrors that of the club. "I became a fan in the off-season of 1966," she said. "My parents discouraged me from being in any sports except gymnastics. In those days, girls didn't play sports."

Raised in Brookline and "only four stops from Fenway" on the Green Line, Giffin thought she'd impress the boy across the street by learning about his favorite team, the Red Sox.

Discouraged from asking questions by her father, "I started to learn about it secretly," Giffin said, going to the library to read up on the game and the team. With a $1 bleacher ticket, Giffin skipped school and went by herself to Opening Day of the '67 season.

"From that point on, I was positively hooked," she said. "I fell in love with the game and dumped the guy."

Giffin got into the club with the help of Sox legend Dom DiMaggio. "We used to get into these great baseball discussions," she said of phone calls with the former centerfielder, who was a client of the insurance company she worked for in the mid-'70s.

"He said, `You should join the Bosox Club, but I'm not sure they let girls in yet.' That was in the day when lady fans were still in the closet," said Giffin.

Through a ticket lottery, Giffin even managed to attend the 1975 World Series for you guessed it Game 6 when catcher Carlton Fisk hit a walkoff home run in the 12th inning to tie the series.

Since '67, Giffin has gone to every Opening Day game and these days hits Fenway every weekend the team is in town, often solo. Her husband, Dave, is also a fan, but is perfectly happy watching the games in the high-tech "sports room" of their Randolph home. The couple spend two weeks in Florida every March during spring training and follow the team around the country at least twice each season.

"We just love the Red Sox. It's something we really enjoy," she said. "It's like a huge family." Giffin is also a longtime member of Sons of Sam Horn, an exclusive online Sox fan board, arranging for 200 of them to attend a Sox game in May.

Despite the team's ups and downs this season and Nomar Garciaparra's departure, Giffin still holds out hope that her favorites, Trot Nixon ("a real get-down, get-dirty" hero), Gabe Kapler ("ooh, those muscles"), and Curt Schilling ("how could you not" be a fan?) can finally bring home a championship.

"They're not gonna kill me," said Giffin. "They may make me feel bad sometimes, but I just love it."

To join the Bosox Club, you must be at least 18 and sponsored by two members. [120]

The Newton Marriott was the site for the September 2004 luncheon; Jason Varitek was named the Man of the Year.

On October 17, David Laurila wrote a piece on club member and longtime (four decades) bleacherite Anne Quinn, which ran in the *Globe*.[121]

It will be noted that later in October, the Red Sox won the World Series — indeed, for the first time since 1918.

Down three-games-to-none in the American League Championhip Series against the New York Yankees, the Red Sox won two extra-inning ballgames at Fenway, then took Games Six and Seven at Yankee Stadium. And then they swept the World Series against the St. Louis Cardinals in four games, extracting some measure of revenge for Game Seven losses in both 1946 and 1967. This was considered a noteworthy event in Red Sox history, and savored by BoSox Club members. Some members were even seen roaming the streets of Kenmore Square in the early morning hours after the final win in St. Louis, and were there to welcome the Red Sox buses at Fenway as they rolled in from Logan Airport around 6 AM.

Ignatius "Kelly" Giglio was among those who were able to savor the long-awaited championship. He had been a Red Sox season ticket holder since 1935 (!) — some 70 years. He had also been a member of the BoSox Club. Kelly Giglio died in the spring of 2005.[122] One of his sons, Richard, was an organist at Fenway Park for a number of years.[123]

On the 40th anniversary of the Club, Red Sox writer Rod Oreste wrote four paragraphs on the club, under the headline "The BoSox Club — 40 Years and Counting." He wrote:

> In 1967, Red Sox broadcaster Ken Coleman joined with Red Sox director of public relations Bill Crowley and en-listed former ballplayers Dom DiMaggio, Ted Lepcio, Frank Malzone and Dick Donovan to form a booster club that became known as The BoSox Club. The creation of such a club would not have been as successful without the voice of Red Sox fans involved.
>
> "After the 1966 season and the low attendance at Fenway Park," says former Red Sox infielder and one-time BoSox Club president Ted Lepcio, "we knew that we wanted to get fans

excited about the Red Sox again and provide a place where fans could gather in support of their team. We based our club on a successful booster club in Cleveland called the Wahoo Club."

Today, the BoSox Club, with approximately 800 members is the oldest and largest booster club of its kind in Major League Baseball. The club's mission remains the same: An organization that serves as the voice of Red Sox fans, promotes baseball at all levels, and assists the Red Sox in community and charitable endeavors."[124]

As the Red Sox celebrate the anniversary of the 1967 Impossible Dream team, they will also honor the anniversary of a first-class organization that has embedded itself in Red Sox tradition.

Note: Donovan was not a ballplayer with the Red Sox, but had played three seasons for the Boston Braves.

Red Sox President & CEO Larry Lucchino added at the time, "The BoSox Club has upheld the great traditions of the Boston Red Sox, and our loyal fans, for the past forty years."

As it happens, the Red Sox won the World Series again in 2007, sweeping the Colorado Rockies in four games. Red Sox fans had nothing against the Rockies, but they stood between the Red Sox and another World Championship.

Burce Donahue was president of the BoSox Club beginning in 2007 and he initiated a new program, inviting 2-4 active-duty members of the armed services to attend BoSox Club luncheons. He personally secured funding from a member who lived in Colorado, who supported the program each year until 2015. Beginning that year, Bruce found another sponsor who is a member and owns a mortgage company. Each of the two donors prefer to remain anonymous, but the guests who attend each luncheon are very appreciative of the invitation and are always welcomed by members with a standing ovation as they are introduced before the meal.

When Jim Rice was inducted into the National Baseball Hall of Fame at Cooperstown, the BoSox Club mounted a special trip for Club members for July 25/26, 2009. Paul Boghosian of the club recalled organizing the trip:

"In 2009 during a spring board meeting of the BoSox club, I asked Dick Bresciani whether the Red Sox would cooperate with the BoSox Club for a club road trip that would allow our members close proximity to Jim Rice and other Red Sox players who would be participating at the ceremony. Dick said that he would see what he could do but naturally made no promises as Rice's schedule would be very full during that time.

"He put me in contact with the bus company that handles all Red Sox local transportation—the Brush Hill Bus Company. From that point on with the blessing of the BoSox Club directors I created an invitation which I sent to members soliciting their interest in an overnight trip to Cooperstown. I coordinated the itinerary with Jeff Idelson of the Hall of Fame, who put me in contact with Shawn Gahagan, VP of Hall of Fame and June Dolhun, Manager of Sales. I believe it cost around $200.

"We booked 30 rooms at a Best Western about 15 or 20 miles from Cooperstown. About 40 members participated in the trip. I arranged for the bus to leave from Fenway and also to pick up members in Framingham. We left the day before the Rice induction. The package involved tickets to the induction in the VIP section, a tour of the Hall of Fame, overnight accommodations, and an ice cream social that I organized to take place following the induction at a recommended Cooperstown venue.

"Dick Bresciani came by and spoke at the social. I was also able to attract Nick Cafardo and I believe Bob Ryan to speak as well. A good time was had by all, alas without the participation by Jim Rice or other players who attended the induction."[125]

Club president Jim Hackett launched Latino Recognition Day in June 2001, with Pedro Martinez as the Club's special guest.

Another guest from another team was Ken Harrelson, White Sox broadcaster (and a member of the 1967 Red Sox), at the May 2002 luncheon.

Twenty years after retirement, Carl Yastrzemski came to the August 2003 luncheon.

Massachusetts Gov. Mitt Romney addressed the September 25, 2003 luncheon.

Tommy Harper and Jerry Remy flank Red Sox photographer Jack Maley at the September 2003 luncheon.

Johnny Pesky's birthday cake, September 2003. Only after his death was it revealed that he had been born in February and not September.

Uri Berenguer of the Red Sox Spanish Radio Network helped psych up David Ortiz for another run at the pennant. May 28, 2004.

Just a month before the Red Sox won their first World Championship in 86 years, Dick Flavin and team captain Jason Varitek regaled members.

The Jimmy Fund has been a longtime beneficiary of BoSox Club charitable efforts. Here Lisa Scherber accepts a check from the Club. L to R: Jimmy Fund Chairman Mike Andrews, Ed Keohane, Scherber, Jean Brooks, Bill Brooks. August 2005.

Peter Gammons, Jerry Remy, Don Orsillo. Three masters of the media visit the Club during the 2007 World Championship season.

Suni Williams and Michael Lopez-Alegria, with Larry Lucchino 12 Nov 2007:
Astronauts Sunita "Suni" Williams and Michael Lopez-Alegria, flew this Red
Sox pennant around the world several times. They are greeted by Sox President
Larry Lucchino at the November 12, 2007 luncheon, all basking in the glow of
that year's World Series sweep.

Dave O'Brien and Rico Petrocelli at the podium, August 24, 2010.

Into the Second Decade of the 21st Century

In 2012, the year that Fenway Park turned 100, the BoSox Club played an active role in the United States Postal Service issuing a postage stamp depicting Ted Williams, who had been deceased the requisite 10 years. Bruce Donahue helped lead the effort. Over 500,000 Ted Williams stamps were pre-ordered by the general public. The first day cover was issued at Cooperstown, and Bruce was present for that ceremony.

On July 21, in a pregame ceremony at Fenway Park, Stephen Dukeman of the BoSox Club was among those on the field for the unveiling of the stamp design.

The following year remains one celebrated by Red Sox fans around the world—in 2013, the Red Sox won yet another World Championship, their third in a 10-year span.

On Dick Bresciani's passing at the end of November in 2014, his obituary noted, "Among his many roles with the Red Sox, Mr. Bresciani coordinated the selection of the annual national Tony Conigliaro Award winner, presented to a Major League player who has overcome adversity. He was the liaison to the BoSox Club, the team's booster club, and was chairman of the Red Sox task force for the 1999 All-Star Game that featured the final appearance of Ted Williams at Fenway Park."[126]

Red Sox President Sam Kennedy—named as such in October 2015 - had a lifelong love for the ballclub. His father, Rev. Thomas B. Kennedy, was a longtime member of the BoSox Club who used to take Sam to the Fenway Park as a child.[127] Sam spoke at a BoSox Club luncheon early in 2016.

The club was also pleased to have the usual array of guests attend luncheons throughout the season, including Man of the Year Rick Porcello at the September luncheon, pitcher David Price and slugger

Jim Rice at the Fenway Park luncheon, and others ranging from new broadcaster Tim Neverett to players Brad Ziegler and Matt Barnes, Christian Vasquez and Sam Horn, to 2004 alumni Orlando Cabrera and Lenny DiNardo, and the ever-popular Luis Tiant. Hosts included Tom Caron, Tom Lydon, Dave O'Brien, and Dan Roche, and of course Dick Flavin was often called upon to treat us to a recent rhyme. There were very enjoyable outings to see the Lowell Spinners play (in Lowell) and the Pawtucket Red Sox play (in Pawtucket.) Thanks as always to Pam Kenn and Sheri Rosenberg for bringing Red Sox guests to the luncheons.

Rear, L to R: Bruce Donahue, Stephen Fife, Dave Joppe, Anthony Rizzo, Will Middlebrooks, Reymond Fuentes, Joel Leonard, Steve Dukeman.
Front: Craig McNaught, Mike Vining.
Photo by Alicia Vining. Spring training 2010.

Every year, the Club sponsors a number of youths to go to a baseball game. Dustin Pedroia greets campers on August 2, 2011.

The Ted Williams postage stamp, issued on July 2, 2012.

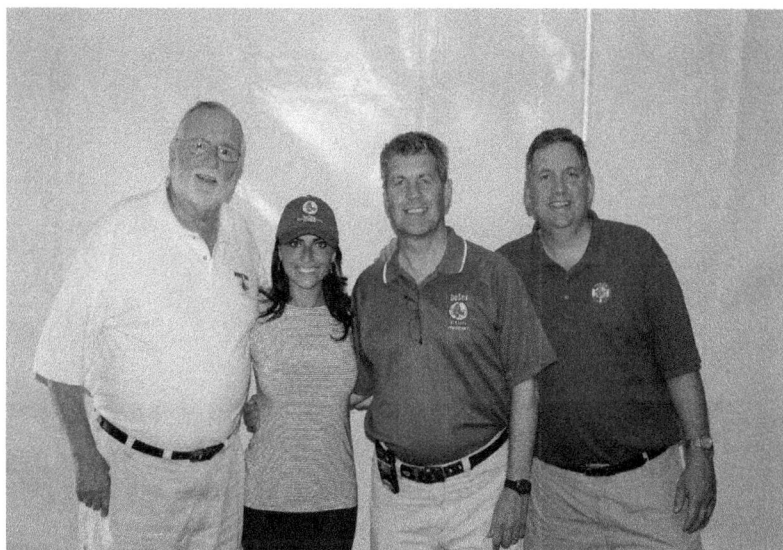

Spring training 2013, L to R: Bruce Donahue, Jenny Dell, Paul Shorthose, and Mike Vining.

Mike Napoli of the Red Sox poses with three United States Marines, the Club's guests at the May 28, 2013 luncheon.

A couple of months before the Red Sox won the World Series, GM Ben Cherington visited the BoSox Club on August 28, 2013.

Dan Roche chats with a legend, Luis Tiant, April 8, 2014.

Family Day at Fenway, July 29, 2014. Craig Breslow takes a question from a kid.

Dan Butler signs a ball for Club member. August 15, 2014.

Dick Flavin declaims about something. November 11, 2015.

Frank Fiorentino and Jean Brooks with the Good Guy Award, while a horde of distinguished well-wishers look on.

Spring training barbecue, 2014. First row, L to R: Danny Mars, Michael Chavis, Kevin McAvoy, Jamie Callahan, Luis Diaz. Second row: Rich Gedman, Debbie Corteau, Cheri Giffin, Bob Rousell, Mike Vining, Bruce Donahue.

Dwight Evans and Joe Castiglione, August 18, 2015.

Red Sox President Sam Kennedy talks at a Club luncheon, November 11, 2015.

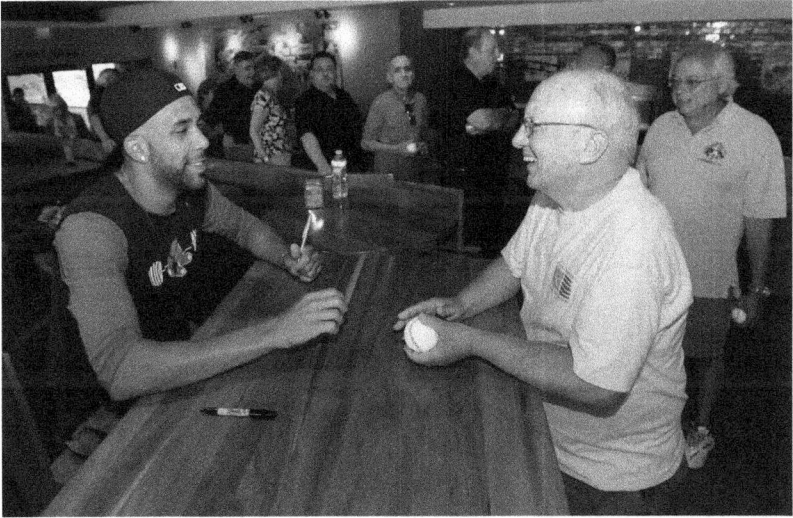

David Price signs items for Club members at the annual Fenway Park luncheon, July 20, 2016.

A guest of the club and Hall of Famer Jim Rice, at the 2016 Fenway Park luncheon.

Jackie Bradley Jr. and Dan Roche field questions at Family Day, July 26, 2016.

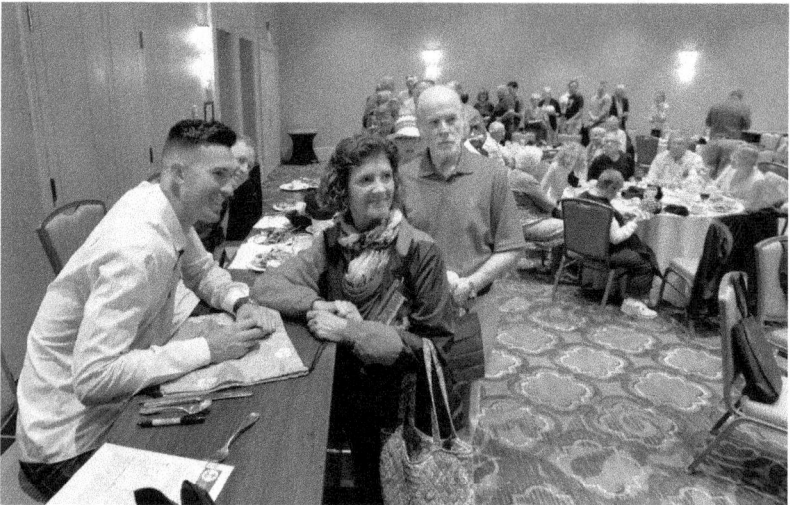

Cy Young Award winner Rick Porcello graciously signs items for a line of well-wishers at the September 13, 2016 luncheon.

BoSox Club executive secretary Beth Donahue Smith with Cy Award winner Rick Porcello, 2016.

BoSox Club Man of the Year

Each year, the BoSox Club awards the BoSox Man of the Year award to a deserving team member recognizing not only their contribution to the success of the team on the field, but also for their cooperation and efforts in community endeavors.

1967 - Rico Petrocelli
1968 - Mike Andrews
1969 - Lee Stange
1970 - Gerry Moses
1971 - John Kennedy
1972 - Bob Montgomery
1973 - Tommy Harper
1974 - Rick Miller
1975 - Denny Doyle
1976 - Reggie Cleveland
1977 - Butch Hobson
1978 - Bill Campbell
1979 - Tom Burgmeier
1980 - Steve Renko
1981 - Jerry Remy
1982 - Bob Stanley
1983 - Carl Yastrzemski
1984 - Mike Easler
1985 - Wade Boggs
1986 - Marty Barrett
1987 - Bruce Hurst
1988 - Bill Fischer
1989 - Dennis Lamp
1990 - Tony Pena

1991 - Tony Fossas
1992 - Roger Clemens
1993 - Mo Vaughn
1994 - Ken Ryan
1995 - Tim Naehring
1996 - Heathcliff Slocumb
1997 - Wendell Kim
1998 - Tim Wakefield
1999 - Trot Nixon
2000 - John Harrington
2001 - Ben Mondor
2002 - Carlos Baerga
2003 - Ron Jackson
2004 - Jason Varitek
2005 - Mike Timlin
2006 - Gabe Kapler
2007 - Kevin Youkilis
2008 - Manny Delcarmen
2009 - Mike Lowell
2010 - Clay Buchholz
2011 - Jed Lowrie
2012 - Jarrod Saltalamacchia
2013 - Craig Breslow
2014 - Victor Rodriguez
2015 - Brock Holt
2016 - Rick Porcello

BoSox Club Presidents

Dom DiMaggio 1967-68
Brad Jernegan 1969-70
Ted Lepcio 1971-72
Bob Cheyne 1973-74
Harry Carlson 1975-76
Clarence March 1977-78
John Busfield 1979-80
Carlo Lagrotteria 1981-82
Jerry Jernegan 1983-84
Lee Cummings 1985-86
George Berardi 1987-88
Frank Geischecker 1989-90
Tom Feenan 1991-92
Tim Dugal 1993-94
Dick Vaughan 1995-96
Craig MacNaught 1997-98
Bill Brooks 1999-2000
Jim Hackett 2001-02
Cheri Giffin 2003-04
Ed Keohane 2005-06
Bruce Donahue 2007-08
Joel Leonard 2009-10
Stephen Dukeman 2011-12
Paul Shorthose 2013-14
Stephen Hollingsworth 2015-16
Mike Vining 2017

The Jernegan Award

The Jernegan Award is named in honor of the late Brad Jernegan, a charter member and President of the BoSox Club in 1969 and 1970. His dedication and tireless efforts on behalf of the BoSox Club remain an inspiration to all that follow. His enthusiasm during the founding of the club and his leadership during the formative years were indispensable to the ultimate success of the Club. The Award, presented by a vote of the Board of Directors, recognizes special and continuing contributions to the BoSox Club. The Award is presented at the Annual Meeting of the BoSox Club in the years in which the Board of Directors believes there is a fitting and deserving candidate. The objective is that the award be given annually.

1972 - Ken Coleman
1973 - Bill Crowley
1974 - *No Award Given*
1975 - *No Award Given*
1976 - Dick Casey
1977 - *No Award Given*
1978 - *No Award Given*
1979 - Harry Carlson
1980 - Dan Campbell
1981 - *No Award Given*
1982 - *No Award Given*
1983 - Buddy LeRoux & Haywood Sullivan
1984 - Bob Cheyne
1985 - Clarence March
1986 - Ted Lepcio
1987 - Tom Feenan, Sr.
1988 - Dr. Jerry Jernegan
1989 - Dick Bresciani
1990 - Mike Ryan

1991 - Bob Stanley
1992 - George Berardi
1993 - Frank Geishecker
1994 - James 'Lou' Gorman
1995 - Tom Feenan, Jr.
1996 - John Harrington
1997 - Audrey Prihoda
1998 - Lee Cummings
1999 - Tim Dugal & Lib Dooley
2000 - Jean Brooks
2001 - Bill Brooks
2002 - *No Award Given*
2003 - Ben Mondor
2004 - Frank Fiorentino
2005 - Craig MacNaught
2006 - Dick Flavin
2007 - Dominic DiMaggio
2008 - Ed Keohane
2009 - Bruce Donahue
2010 - Johnny Pesky
2011 - Cynthia Geoff
2012 - Dr. Joel Leonard
2013 - Stephen Dukeman
2014 - Dan Roche
2015 - Paul Shorthose
2016 - Larry Lucchino

A Summary Look at Fan and Booster Clubs Around Major-League Baseball

Anaheim Angels

Tim Mead of the Angels introduced us to Darlene Oliveira, a longtime member of the Angels Booster Club, who provided us a history of the club. Gene Autry purchased the Angels in 1961 as a major-league expansion team. Despite being a new franchise, the Angels Booster Club is actually three years older than the BoSox Club.

Darlene writes, "In 1964, three years later, the Angels Booster Club was established and began holding meetings at a restaurant in Anaheim. Mr. Autry was a huge supporter of our Booster Club and would sometimes sing at the Club events. The Boosters have supported the Angels through the ups and downs to a World Series win in 2002. Boosters have also seen many changes in names, ownership, uniforms, and mascots. As additional proof of our continuing support, the Booster Club has had season seats for over 30 years. Our Club now holds their meetings once a month at Angel Stadium. In 2014, the Angels Booster Club proudly celebrated their 50th Anniversary.

"The Boosters have always had a close relationship with the team. Booster members would go to Spring Training when it was in Palm Springs, California, and now in Tempe, Arizona.

"The Boosters handed out promotional items at home games for over 20 years. They attend home and away games as a group, have game watch parties, and Player Luncheons where our members can

Members of the Angels Booster Club volunteering at an RBI event, 2016.

meet established or up-and-coming players, coaches and broadcasters. When the franchise was newer, the Boosters would sponsor picnics where players would umpire softball games between the Boosters and players' families. There would also be a Wives/Girlfriends Luncheon to honor the support of the women behind the players. At the end of the year, Boosters would have a party for the players and their families.

"Angels Booster members continue to proudly support our community by sponsoring an annual Toy and School Supply Drive. Our members also assist the American Red Cross with their Annual Blood Drive. Angels Boosters also support organizations with events such as Food Drives, Run/Walk fundraisers, RBI League, and other events to help disadvantaged youth and members of our local community. For the past two years we have volunteered at the Light the Night Walk sponsored by the Leukemia & Lymphoma Society held at Angel Stadium. Every year we continue to expand our community involvement and other charitable endeavors. Our motto is 'Helping Others through the Love of Angels Baseball.' We look forward to continuing our support of Angels Baseball for many years to come!"

The luncheons vary in price, depending on the venue and the choice of food, but the goal is to keep them affordable to all.

The Boosters fluctuate between 180 and 220 members, with a third to a half of the membership attending the monthly general meetings. Those meetings, at the stadium, are free to members who pay an annual fee of $30 ($20 for each additional adult in the household). Out of state membership is a flat $20 per household. Children are $5.

The membership is varied in age, from retirees to younger members. At the meetings, Darlene explains, "We usually have speakers that include someone in the community or from the Angels Organization. We have also had artists, writers, and retired ballplayers who are an inspiration to others through their love of baseball and Angels baseball."

A look at the Angels website indicates that the Angels themselves don't seem to have any other form of fan clubs, not even the sort of one oriented toward children that is common with other teams.

Thanks to Todd Anton, Tim Mead, and Darlene Oliveira.

Arizona Diamondbacks

There was a website with the URL dbackfans.com, but the ownership of the domain had expired by September 2016. An email sent to Jacob Pomrenke of the Society for American Baseball Research (headquartered in Phoenix) elicited the following response:

"I've never heard anything around here about any type of D'backs fan club like those. What you see more of these days are the team-oriented fan blogs, like AZ Snake Pit: http://www.azsnakepit.com/. That's a real community, entirely online, but two of their writers often contribute articles to the Gameday program at D'backs games."

The AZ Snake Pit site is part of the SB Nation collection of blogs, though they have been known to have the occasional meetup such as the one for Game #160 on September 30, 2016—a home game against the Padres—dubbed SnakePit Fest 2016. Based on the frequency of posts to the Snake Pit site (apparently only a few per month), it's not a very active site.

Jacob writes, "The other main D'backs fan site, which is affiliated with ESPN's Sweetspot network, is Inside the 'Zona. The two guys who run that site also contribute articles to the Gameday program at home games." The site is at http://insidethezona.com and the two guys are Ryan P. Morrison (originally from Boston) and Jeff Wiser (originally from Oregon). They also maintain @InsidetheZona on Twitter as a site account and are on Facebook at https://www.facebook.com/insidethezona.

In an email on October 20, 2016, Jim McLennan of the Snake Pit writes, "I started writing about the D-backs in 2003, mostly as a coping mechanism so my poor wife wouldn't have to listen to me rant. :) That site became part of SB Nation in 2005, and has been growing ever since. It is much more of an online forum than a physical one: we have members all over the world, including Brazil, England and, for a while, even in China.

"All told, there are just shy of 5,000 registered users, though it's not necessary to register in order to read content, only if you want to comment, post your own articles, etc. Over the past month, September 2016, Google Analytics tells me we've had about 42,500 unique visitors to the site. However, in terms of regular active participants, the numbers are naturally much smaller, with a couple of hundred likely responsible for the bulk of activity.

"We have had various get-togethers: generally, there's one in spring training, one in the regular season and then another for the Arizona Fall League. These are almost entirely informal affairs: organization largely consists of picking a date, and then people showing up!

"On the online front, we have a Gameday Thread for every game, a post in which members can hang out, comment on proceedings as it unfolds. These can be pretty sizable; the last time the D-backs made the postseason (in 2011), the Game Five NLDS resulted in over 3,000 comments. However, there hasn't been any such cause for much excitement lately among D-backs fans, and the typical game this year was probably between 300-500."

Unlike most of the other major-league teams, the Diamondbacks don't seem to have organized their own fan clubs, not even for kids—though there are a number of ways kids can participate in activities at times throughout the season. One such is the D-backs Baseball Academy, which takes advantage of the Arizona climate and "offers youth baseball and softball camps all year long." The price for participation is $100.

Thanks to Jacob Pomrenke and Jim McLennan.

Atlanta Braves

Braves 400 Fan Club

Even before the Braves arrived in Atlanta from Milwaukee, they had a booster club in place—the 400 Club, founded during a meeting at the Capri Motel on March 24, 1965. On the club's 50th anniversary, in 2015, Wayne Coleman put together a pamphlet: *50 Years of Supporting Braves Baseball.* Joe Gerson, an insurance executive, was the first president of the 400 Club. In remembering that initial meeting, Gerson said, "There were eight or ten of us there—Steve Schmidt, Al Thompson, Jack Vax, J.L. Jerden, the late Ed Harris and Georgia Tech baseball coach Joe Pittard. Representing the Braves were Bill Bartholomay, Chairman of the Board, and Eddie Glennon, General Manager of the Atlanta Crackers and 400 Club visionary."

The goal was to enroll 400 members, but it rapidly reached 600. In 1967, the club began a tradition of honoring local high school baseball players at one of their luncheons. They have continued to work closely with the Boys Club in the area, providing gifts of baseball equipment. Club members brought a little muscle to help go with their donations and helped build a softball field at the Devereux Center in Marietta, a behavioral health treatment center for youth.

They hosted visiting teams at luncheons—one in 1969 drew over 250 fans, who saw Pirates Roberto Clemente, Willie Stargell and several others. Each year they give out various awards such as Player of the Year, Rookie of the Year, and even Fan of the Year. The list of players attending their luncheons — including former Braves even going back to the Boston Braves — is staggering. It is very impressive and far too extensive to include here.

The club has also mounted road trips to Wrigley Field, and to San Francisco. In 1990, a Braves Baseball Barnstorming Bus Tour in July took Club members to three Braves minor-league games within 48 hours, in South Carolina, Virginia, and North Carolina. In later years, the club has taken trips to Baltimore, St, Louis, Houston, Pittsburgh, Milwaukee, Boston, Washington, and other cities, some of them more than once.

In January 1991, over 600 people attended the 25th Annual Eddie Glennon Gameboree at the Radisson Hotel Atlanta. The club has also organized trips to Cooperstown to see Braves greats such as in 2014 to see Greg Maddux and Tom Glavine inducted into the Hall of Fame.

Each September the 400 Club holds a "Call-Up Luncheon," always well attended, to welcome the new Braves rookies to the major leagues.

Club members volunteered to help the ballclub at the time Atlanta hosted the All-Star Game, at World Series events, and more.

The Braves ballclub, appreciative of the support of the club over the years, accorded 400 Club members the opportunity to purchase postseason tickets.

Dues to join the 400 Club dues are $25 per year, then a reduced amount for each additional family member. Membership is open to anyone, no invitation or member recommendation needed. Membership had grown at one point to close to 1,600, but has settled back down to around 400-500.

The club maintains a website at www.braves400.org, which offers the opportunity to learn more about one of baseball's most active and successful fan clubs.

Thanks to Tom Hufford.

Baltimore Orioles

Although a major-league franchise was only born again in 1953 when the St. Louis Browns moved to Baltimore, it didn't take long for a booster club to spring up as well.

As the Oriole Advocates explain on their website, "A long long time ago, Baltimoreans were enjoying the seventh season of the city's return to major league baseball when nine local businessmen envisioned a need for a volunteer organization that would promote the sort on both the professional and amateur levels.

After several feasibility meetings, the group extended invitations to other area businessmen to join the organization. The first formal meeting of the baseball enthusiasts was held on July 9, 1960, at Memorial Stadium, and was attended by 25 individuals, including three officials of the Baltimore Orioles. They named themselves The Oriole Advocates and they characterized themselves as "an organization of volunteers joined together to promote and stimulate an interest in baseball at all levels, among youths of all ages."

See the site at:

http://www.orioleadvocates.org/

Their first activity was Camera Day in 1961, which allowed fans to photograph their favorite players on the infield at Memorial Stadium. In 1976, the Advocates collaborated with the Orioles team to found the Orioles Hall of Fame. Other collaborations have included Little League clinics, and — in 1962 — the O's Dugout Club, which over the years has enrolled over a quarter-million members aged 16 or younger. Needless to say, many of those younger fans remain partisans of the Orioles today.

In 1967, the Advocates began work to restore the Baltimore house where Babe Ruth was born and transform it into the Babe Ruth Museum it is today.

Since the program began in 1992, the Cardboard to Leather program has gathered more than 80 tons of baseball equipment to youth organizations in Afghanistan, Aruba, Belize, Cuba, Dominican Republic, Ghana, Iraq, Nicaragua, and Venezuela.

Like many ballclubs, the Orioles offer giveaway premiums to ticketed fans—think bobbleheads, t-shirts, and even an O's BBQ spatula. The men and women of the Advocates are the ones who help distribute these items to arriving fans. It is said to be the longest-running cooperative effort between the ballclub and the Oriole Advocates.

Thanks to Kristen Hudak of the Orioles, and Dr. Charles Steinberg.

Boston Red Sox

The story of the "organic" Red Sox fan and booster clubs—including the BoSox Club—is told elsewhere in this volume. The Red Sox also have clubs they have established on their own. The largest and most successful of these is Red Sox Nation. Annual membership is currently $14.95, and includes similar features to other teams' clubs, such as a discount on Team Store purchases, MLB Gameday audio, a decal, and a personalized membership card. It also includes early access to games, permitting Red Sox Nation members to watch early batting practice from atop the Green Monster (and maybe catch a ball.) They have also recently added another tier of RSN membership for free.

Red Sox Kid Nation offers two levels of membership—a rookie membership which is free, and an All-Star membership which costs $39.95 (more than double Red Sox Nation membership, but this gets those 14 and under a free t-shirt, an LED watch, a backpack, and a free ticket to a Red Sox game, as well as other benefits.)

In a June 25, 2016 interview with Dr. Charles Steinberg at McCoy Stadium in Pawtucket, he explained in some depth the origins of Red Sox Nation, providing a rare and candid look into the internal discussions of the philosophy regarding team-organized approaches toward their fans.

"You know that 'Red Sox Nation' is a three-word phrase that already has depth in the marketplace. It's an organic, natural, occurring description of an increasingly worldwide fan base. It exists. We don't start it. We don't create it. We don't invent it. We recognize it. We recognize that it exists.

"2002, 2003. In 2004, we're on top of the world. Now we win the World Series on October 27, 2004. The first week of November, we want to capture that data, to do that census, to discover what we successfully discovered in San Diego to the tune of 140,000. Gosh, how many Red Sox fans are there?

"But there is this strenuous debate in the office. I want to find out, for free, like we did in San Diego…I want you to sign up for free so that we draw the circle around the largest population—and then, once you know that population, you can give them opportunities for purchases.

"There's a different argument being put forth that says in order to do this with technological savvy, you have to do it through BAM. And to do it through BAM, there's going to need to be a fee, and so there's got to be some payment at the start, no matter how small. So, one argument is no, no, no, no, no, keep it free. We were hearing about this fellow in Cambridge who was having success with something that we all now know as Facebook. Free, and he was getting 500 million people. That's valuable. But the other point was no, no, no, you have to pay X. And there's a danger when you have to pay X.

"Suddenly, you're telling people who already know inherently that they are members of Red Sox Nation that they have to pay to be members of Red Sox Nation. That is a contradiction. 'I don't have to pay, because I *am* a member.' But we're saying you have to pay. An organization has to make a judgment on its values, and the people in charge of generating revenue were making an argument about the potential revenue—because we were so hot that altruism and market strategy wasn't competing. We both wanted to know the same thing—to know what is the total population of Red Sox Nation. One way is to let the people tell us that they're members. And the other way is to let them tell us technologically through BAM, and they've got to pay whatever it was - $15.

"Those on the side of not charging were disappointed, but respectful. Those who were on the side of revenue were validated, because not only did you get people signing up but one of the keys to signing up was that you were then in the exclusive company of those who had access to buying tickets that not everybody had access to. But that could drive an altruist even more crazy, because then we were saying 'Pay us, so that you can pay us. Pay us for the right to pay us.' That doesn't feel good. I don't like that as a fan. But the market was bearing that. That was the birth of the club's fan club called Red Sox Nation.

"It started off all right. I remember the number 40,000. Then within that, people also paid for Green Monster seats. Collateral revenue. But I always came back to: 'Really? 40,000?' And then, of course, it dissipated. The team wasn't as good. The demand was lower. And you had to pay. I'm going, '40,000? And we got 140,000 in San Diego?' It illustrates the flaw. But the revenue was undeniable, and so I fully respect those who were in charge of generating the revenue—but I also lamented that we didn't wrap our arms with a hug around the largest possible population. I don't blame them. I just lamented it.

"Then we wanted a children's version. It became....Red Sox Kid Nation. That's what it became, but it was Red Sox....Junior..."club" was the word, and Lucchino talked to his stepson and he said, 'No, we don't want to be in a club.' Red Sox Kid Nation. And it worked. Now, once again, you sold memberships. You sold them, and you got a lot of value, but it was a paid-for fan club.

"Turn the clock ahead to 2014 or 2015, to Sam Kennedy's credit—knowing that children are essential to the future of the club—Sam Kennedy and Adam Grossman made it free. So they did what some had hoped for back in 2004: draw your circle around the biggest population, and then talk to your market. From a kids standpoint, it came back beautifully, and the numbers were robust. The number of kids was maybe 50,000, up from like 12,000. You don't have to put a dollar sign on the front door. Let them in the front door for free, and then let them shop around. That's what Red Sox Kid Nation is a testament to. And Sam Kennedy and Adam Grossman have done that.

"There is a fundamental value of how you approach baseball marketing. If you start with 'you pay me,' you're going to limit your audience. And you're going to limit it in an unhealthy, potentially lucrative way."

Regarding the BoSox Club, Dr. Steinberg had this to add: If you're in my shoes, you love the BoSox Club. There were quiet, good, baseball-loving fans who demonstrated their affection routinely and frequently and loved it. The 35th anniversary of the BoSox Club was our first year at the Red Sox, and Dom DiMaggio—the first president—was present when Bresh, Larry, Dom DiMaggio—I was there, but not part of the picture—affixed the bronze plaque to Fenway for the BoSox Club. We did recognize that, with Dom DiMaggio, in 2002.

"The BoSox Club was almost a neighborhood fan club, while Red Sox Nation was a worldwide census. That's how I would describe the two.

"To me, they're all good. They're all fans. Any fan is doing you a favor by being a fan. *Any* fan is doing you a favor by being a fan. They're all carrying your flag for you. You better not take for granted people who wake up with baseball in their soul."

Red Sox Nation may be found at: http://boston.redsox.mlb.com/bos/fan_forum/redsox_nation.jsp

Red Sox Kid Nation may be found at: http://boston.redsox.mlb.com/bos/fan_forum/kidnation.jsp

Thanks to Dr. Charles Steinberg.

Chicago Cubs

Peter Chase of the Cubs (formerly of the Media Relations crew for the Red Sox) put me in touch with team historian Ed Hartig. I led off by asking Ed about the Emil Verban Society, and received the following detailed response regarding Cubs fan clubs:

"A guy named Bruce Ladd ran the Emil Verban Society. I say ran as it now longer exists (for at least the last 5-6 years, probably longer). Bruce's claim to Cubs fame was that he (or was it his wife) was related to George Pearce (also seen as Pierce), who pitched for the Cubs from 1912-1916.

"Ladd, who was a registered lobbyist, would reach out to any politico with a Chicago connection or interest in baseball to join the society ... with many joining including Hillary Rodham Clinton, President Reagan, Jim Brady, etc. He also sent out invites to broadcasters, writers, actors, Supreme Court Justices, Senators, etc - the membership list was a who's who. Bruce funded the society himself - eventually the work and the cost began to catch up with him - so he eventually put a stop to the EVS.

"The Cubs had no official connection with the Emil Verban Society ... though the club would eventual grow to include Ernie Banks, Billy Williams, Jack Brickhouse.

"I believe the longest running booster club/baseball society in Chicago is the Old Timers' Baseball Association of Chicago - formed in 1919. That club was formed in recognition of the 50th anniversary of the founding of the first professional baseball team in Chicago. I know the club is active - though I don't know how active it is ... it might not be much more than posting old photos to a website.

"The most impacting Cubs booster club was the Die Hard Cubs Fan Club that began in the late 1970s/early 1980s and was officially recognized by the team starting in June 1982. Are you familiar with the Cubs Convention? That actually began as the Die Hard Cubs Fan Club Convention. For the first couple years of the convention, the first and last days of the convention was limited to fan club members only.

"Are you familiar with the Cubs magazine *Vine Line*? It initially was a promo item for the DHCFC with those joining the club receiving the magazine as part of their annual membership.

"The success of the Cubs Convention and *Vine Line* slowly meant the end of the DHCFC. With more and more baseball information being available year round, there wasn't the need for a baseball support system mid-winter.

"In recent years there was a group called the 'Out of Left Field Society' - that group's purpose was to raise awareness of the West Side Grounds, the Cubs home prior to Wrigley Field. That society's goal was to raise money for a marker for the park's site. Once that was accomplished, the group pretty much fizzled away.

"In years lone gone by there were officially recognized kids clubs and well as many, many unofficial clubs for players (Gabby Hartnett had several as did Ron Santo) and announcer (such as Bert Wilson)."

There are currently two team-organized fan clubs:

http://chicago.cubs.mlb.com/chc/fan_forum/cubs_club/details.jsp#contact_us

There is also a Cubs Newborn Fan Club (team organized):

http://chicago.cubs.mlb.com/chc/fan_forum/newborn_fan_club.jsp

One expects that, after winning a World Championship for the first time in 108 years, the clubs may grow. There is, though, the other side of the coin which suggests that some fanbases may thrive in adversity.

Thanks to Peter Chase and Ed Hartig.

Chicago White Sox

The White Sox, like the Cubs, have a team-organized club for children, the White Sox Kids Club. It can be found at:

http://chicago.whitesox.mlb.com/cws/fan_forum/kidsclub_index.jsp

One notes that welcoming new members is apparently not a year-round goal. When the site was accessed in September 2016, a notice was noticed: "Registration for the 2016 White Sox Kids Club is now closed. Check back in November to register for the 2017 Kids Club!"

There doesn't appear to be a fan-generated fan club for the White Sox, but there is a team-organized one called the Sox Pride Club. There are also the usual opportunities to connect with the team through its Social Media Clubhouse, blogs, and fantasy camp, etc. As with the White Sox Kids Club, the Sox Pride Club was no longer accepting memberships in September 2016. A notice on the site said, "2016 SPC memberships are sold out." The Sox Pride Club is located at:

http://chicago.whitesox.mlb.com/cws/fan_forum/spc/index.jsp

The White Sox do have a "Manager of Fan Engagement," who goes by the name of Night Train Veeck.

Cincinnati Reds

There is a very active group in Cincinnati called "The Rosie Reds." Sean Lahman writes that the group "started as a women-only group in the early 1960s, but expanded to include men a few years later. They used to organize groups to follow the Reds on the road. More recently, they're involved in a lot of philanthropic efforts — a scholarship program, I think. An article about them in 2014 said they have about 3,000 members."

The article by John Erardi appeared in the *Cincinnati Enquirer* on July 24, 2014. It began by detailing how in 1964, with Reds owner Bill DeWitt entertaining the idea of moving the franchise to San Diego, the Greater Cincinnati Chamber of Commerce looked to see what could be done to drum up more fan support. Erardi wrote, "A male-dominated 'Committee of 40' businesses was formed, but ultimately it was the women's division of that committee — a group that came to be known as the 'Rosie Reds' — that branched off and proved to have a bigger and more enduring impact."

Within some years, they were even taking road trips, including a convoy of 14 buses that traveled to Pittsburgh to catch a game there in 1972. Indeed, "So good were the Rosies at drawing Big Red Machine players to its functions, that by 1971, men were clamoring to join its ranks."

A winning ballclub always attracts fans, of course. The success on the field of the Big Red Machine in the 1970s truly helped solidify the franchise in Cincinnati.

"Our very first male was Mr. DeWitt himself, because he obviously knew the value of drawing women as far as increasing attendance at the ballpark," Lynne Gibson, past president of the Rosie Reds and now its historian, said to Erardi. The Rosie Reds had worked with the ballpark on parking, and even worked with them to improve the quality of the ice at the park (!), and had their own special seating section at Crosley Field.

They call themselves the longest running fan organization in the major leagues.

Membership has gone up and down, of course, but was capped at 3,000 in 1971 and remains just "a few hundred shy of 3,000" today. Erardi wrote, "The organization is perhaps best known for its trips to other major league parks, and now even minor league parks, such as those in Dayton and Louisville. There was a time when fashion shows by Reds wives were big draws, but those have dropped off as players have become more transient and department stores have greatly reduced their budgets for such shows. The Rosies still award baseball scholarships annually to local universities."

The team even has a Rosie Red mascot, which dates back to 1939.

Benefits of membership include two free tickets to a Guest of the Reds Game, discounted appreciation games throughout the year, ballpark tours, opportunities to purchase postseason tickets, take part in an Opening Day parade, a riverboat cruise, and the opportunity to attend a number of member events and meetings (which are held at the team's Great American Ball Park). And more.

The ballclub itself offers team-organized clubs. As one grows older, there is a new club at various steps along the way. First there is Red Rookies, a "baby club" for children age 3 and under. Then one may progress to the Reds Heads Kids Club, for kids 4 through 12. And there follows Club Red, which caters to fans aged 13-17. Reds Heads membership is $30 annually, but one gets quite a lot: a Reds Heads gym bag, an exclusive Reds sport performance shirt, a Reds spirit cape/wall banner, a Reds Heads pillow case, 5 Reds temporary tattoos, an Official Reds Heads membership card with lanyard, access to ballpark experiences like player autograph sessions and chances to take the field, and—most significantly—two free tickets to any Sunday-Thursday Reds home game. There are also "great offers" from sponsors like the Newport Aquarium, Cincinnati Zoo, Cincinnati Museum Center, Bob Evans, Coney Island, and College Advantage.

Fans seeking romance can take advantage of "Reds Singles"—which, as the Tampa Bay Rays offer their fans, turns out to be a way to connect to the site Match.com where you might find compatible singles who happen to be fans of your ballclub. It may be noted that Match.com offers same-sex dating as well as connections to the opposite sex.

In the half-hearted (if that) department, someone started a "Cincinnati Reds Fanclub" on Facebook, perhaps in October 2013. It has only attracted 24 "likes" in three years, and only posted 10 items in that period of time.

Thanks to Sean Lahman.

Cleveland Indians

The Wahoo Club, founded in 1962, is now into its sixth decade and is recognized by the Cleveland Indians as their official booster club. On their website, www.wahooclub.com, there is a history of the club, and it reads thus:

"Necessity, as the saying goes, is often the mother of invention. And that is how the Wahoo Club came into being.

"In 1962, Cleveland and all of professional baseball was full of speculation that hard times at the turnstiles would force the Indians to abandon the only home they had known throughout their history. It was a history that dated back to 1869 when the Cleveland Forest Citys were born. They, in turn became the Spiders (1889), the Blues (1900), the Broncos (1902), the Naps (1903), and our beloved Indians (1915).

"Greener pastures, it was feared, might soon be found hundreds of miles from the lakefront stadium and its millions of memories.

"As 'save the Indians' stories multiplied in the local media and 'hot stove' conversations, local advertising executive, Leonard Axelband, envisioned grassroots support in the form of an adult boosters club.

"With the cooperation of Gabe Paul, Indians President, and Nate Wallack, the public relations director for the ball club, Mr. Axelband contacted a group of former baseball players and civic leaders with close ties to the sport.

"The list included All-Star third baseman Al Rosen, pitching great Mike Garcia, and I.S. (Nig) Rose, a longtime backer of amateur baseball in the city, as well as John Nagy, Cleveland's nationally known Recreation Director. Hall of Famer Bob Feller and Gordon Cobbledick, long-respected sports editor of *The Plain Dealer*; and local businessmen Tom O'Connell, David Leahy, and Ron Cohen also were early backers of the organization.

"With guidance from these leaders, the organization took shape and grew rapidly. The club took its name from Chief Wahoo, the club's long standing symbol. From the initial 1962 membership of 175, The Wahoo Club had prospered through the years, reaching an annual membership in excess of 1,500 even in 'lean years' where a first division finish for the Indians was only a distant dream. Grassroots interest is real.

"Luncheon meetings through the years have seen most of baseball's brightest stars shine at the speaker's platform, including Pete Rose who was given a special 'Charlie Hustle Award' in 1979. When Bob Feller and Lou Boudreau were elected to Baseball's Hall of Fame, record numbers attended the luncheons to honor the former Tribe heroes. The Wahoo Club is proud of the role it played in helping Bob Lemon into the Hall of Fame. In 1976, the year Bob was elected, they sent fresh lemons to all baseball writers who were eligible to vote.

"Among the proud traditions that have continued through the years is the Gordon Cobbledick Tomahawk Award, given since 1963 to the member of the Indians ball club who has made the most outstanding contribution to his team during the preceding season. It carries a special significance because it is the only award of its kind where the winner is elected by his teammates.

"A second great tradition is a scholarship given each year to a baseball player at Cleveland State University in memory of Luke Easter, former Indian great and longtime member of The Wahoo Board of Directors.

"As the first such booster club in the nation, The Wahoo Club and its members are also proud of the support and guidance they provided in the formation of similar organizations in other major-league cities. We also point with pride to the many Wahoo Clubs scattered throughout the country which were formed by rabid Indians fans who closely follow the Tribe's fortunes from hundreds even thousands of miles away.

"We're proud of this history. Back in 1962, The Wahoo Club was dedicated to a premise: To Further Interest In Baseball On All Levels. Our goal remains the same today. We hope you will join us so that we can further that goal."

Membership dues are modest, with children's membership at $15 and a single adult membership just $25. There are family memberships for $45, and lifetime memberships at $75 for an individual and $100 for a family.

The year 2016 offered a number of events. Prices for the luncheons and dinners typically ranged from $29 to $32 in 2016.

- Wahoo Club Lunch - Talking Tribe w/Special Guests
- Wahoo Club Lunch - 1996 Olympic Silver Medalist Matt Ghaffari
- Wahoo Club Lunch - w/Bob Golic Aug. 28th 2016
- Wahoo Club Lunch - w/Josh Tomlin Aug. 13th, 2016
- Believeland Luncheon with Special Guest Earnest Byner
- Wahoo Club Lunch - w/Trevor Bauer
- Wahoo Club Luncheon w/Carlos Baerga June 18, 2016
- Wahoo Club 1 Day Bus Trip To Detroit Saturday June 25, 2016
- Wahoo Club Dinner with Cleveland Indians Tyler Naquin
- Wahoo Club Salute to the Cleveland Browns
- Wahoo Club Lunch - Josh Cribbs
- Wahoo Club Trip - Philadelphia 4 Day Family Weekend Wahoo

Club president Bob Rosen responded to a few questions in October 2016, and said that the club at the time had 2,217 paid members. In addition to the various events throughout the season, each year the Wahoo Club also brings baseball-oriented gifts to the local children's hospitals. The luncheons are typically first come/first served to the first 150 who respond.

There is also a team-organized club for kids, Tribe Town MVPs. It is described as the "official kids fan club of the Cleveland Indians." For $20, one can get "One-of-a-kind Tribe Gear" including a replica jersey (one size fits all), souvenir baseball, drawstring bag, lanyard, and membership badge. You get $10.00 loaded value onto a card you can use to buy from concession stands at the ballpark (that's half the price back right there!), as well as "invitations to exclusive experiences like: MVP Batting Practice Viewing Sessions on the field, Catch on the Field after select home games, Meet and greet with Slider and the Hot Dogs, Leading the Line when kids run the bases after all Sunday home games."

Thanks to Stephanie Liscio and Joe Wancho.

Colorado Rockies

Paul Parker of SABR, the team historian for the Rockies wrote, "We do not have an official fan or booster club, other than the Rockies Rookies fan club for kids, 15 and under.

"There are blogs out there, but I wouldn't characterize them clubs of the equivalent of the BoSox Club."

The Rockies Rookies club (which even includes a toddlers club for dedicated fans, ages 1 through 3) can be visited at:

http://colorado.rockies.mlb.com/col/fan_forum/kidsclub.jsp

Thanks to Paul Parker.

Detroit Tigers

Tigers fan Mark Pattison writes: "Well, there IS the Mayo Smith Society for Tigers fans, founded in 1983 in Washington, D.C. We had our annual gathering in 2016, and all three co-founders were there to talk about the early days. There is (or should be) an abbreviated history of the Society on our new website, www.mayosmithsociety.org.

"Also more modern than Mayo Smith (as a society), there's the invitation-only Eddie Lake Society based in Detroit, which gets together for lunch every quarter or so. For details, get in touch with Karen Elizabeth Bush at lexiconsvs@aol.com.

"There's even a Detroit Baseball Society, but it seems to be for guys who want to have a big-ticket charity dinner with a ballplayer or two. I searched for them online last month. I can't remember any of the particulars, though."

Visiting the Tigers' own website in late September 2016, one finds the "2013 Official Detroit Tigers Fan Club Presented by Muller Lite Benefits." It is at: http://detroit.tigers.mlb.com/det/fan_forum/fan-club_details.jsp

One is entitled to items fans might not reasonably want, such as "2013 MLB.com Gameday Audio for your computer." In fact, it's a reasonably safe bet that today's Boston Red Sox fans would rather listen to 2013 Gameday Audio than Tigers fans, particularly the 2013 American League Championship Series. There is something about Shane Victorino's grand slam in the bottom of the seventh inning in the Game Seven 5-2 win at Fenway Park that might more likely appeal to Red Sox fans.

Tigers Kids, on the other hand, at http://detroit.tigers.mlb.com/det/fan_forum/kids_index.jsp was already offering information on 2017 memberships.

Thanks to Mark Pattison.

Houston Astros

Though it exists no more, the Astros Orbiters were the original booster club for the Houston Astros. Mike Acosta, the team's manager of authentication, referred an inquiry to former Orbiters president Babs Cannon, who in an October 17 interview told a bit about the club.

She was president twice, a true fan who said that she only missed two home games in the first five years she had season tickets. Karen

Williams was a 22-year-old intern in the Astros' front office and one of the things they told her to do was, "Organize a booster club."

"In the beginning, when we were getting organized," Babs said, "Karen kept setting up meetings at this local pub, a local sports bar. And no one was coming to the meetings, so she finally ask, 'What's going on?' She was told, 'Well, most of us in this group are Southern Baptists and we don't drink.' So she changed the location.

"We had six luncheons. We had a luncheon a month during the season, and we chose a player and a pitcher of the month. They were invited. And then other players. We had a visiting team person come, too. Milo Hamilton was the MC at all of our luncheons when I was president and for many years.

"We regularly had two or three hundred at the luncheons. We'd give each member an Astros Orbiters t-shirt when they joined the booster club plus a subscription to the tabloid *Astrosports.* Club membership fee was originally $15, and then $12.50 to renew. The luncheons usually ranged $8 to $9, just depending on what we were doing at the time. We would have them at local hotels, usually close to the ballpark, for the players [ease of travel.]" There were usually 200 to 300 people at each luncheon."

The club helped raised charitable funds, and helped sponsor the baseball program at San Jacinto Junior College; it also donated money to Alvin Community College.

"I had 785 members in my last term in '86. We put a limit on our club, because we didn't have the capabilities. With 1,500 members, we'd have more people than we could handle at the luncheons. They wouldn't have a chance to really meet the players. We limited it to 1,000." Former president Natalie Harris, a New York transplant, explained to *Houston* magazine that it could well have grown to around 4,000, but "I wanted it to be something special" where luncheon attendees could actually have a chance to meet the players.

Though the Astros had boosted the idea of a booster club, they then stepped back and took no official role in the operations of the club. Williams became a front-office employee and later married outfielder Billy Hatcher.

The group had since dissolved. Babs believes that was in the mid to late 1990s. She's not aware of any other groups since that time. She dates her memory of when it was dissolved through one recollection. "Milo Hamilton was the announcer for the Astros from '86 or something. He passed away last year. After I retired [from her work with Conoco] in 2002, he told me, 'Babs, when you retire, your goal in life is to resurrect the booster club.' I said, 'Read my lips - No.' I'd been through that, and it was like 24/7. I had done my share.

"I loved it back when it started. I really wish somehow that the younger fans would maybe do something like that again."

A look at "Astros Fan Central" on the current Astros website shows a Social Media Clubhouse, offers the opportunity to buy commemorative bricks, has an "Astros Singles" dating site (the link goes to Match.com, but presumably the Astros derive some material benefit from the link), and tells you how to get the Shuttle Crew to your event or have your holiday photo taken with Orbit, the team mascot. There is no team-run fan club.

Thanks to Mike Acosta and Babs Cannon.

Kansas City Royals

After the Kansas City Royals won the American League pennant in 2014, Lynn Horsley of the *Kansas City Star* wrote, "Some of the Kansas City Royals' most loyal supporters have been the longtime members of the Royal Lancers, who sold season tickets and sustained the fan base through good years and many bad years."

Soon after Ewing and Muriel Kauffman founded the team in 1968, explained Curt Nelson of the Royals Hall of Fame, they knew something needed to be done to generate sales. "The backbone of every franchise is season ticket sales. With Kauffman's knack for salesmanship, it wasn't surprising that Ewing and Muriel together quickly sold nearly 3,000 season tickets themselves. But they knew the job was too big for them alone.

"Kauffman borrowed aspects of an elite sales club at Marion Labs to create the Royal Lancers, a group of area business professionals who served as an unpaid sales force of baseball ambassadors throughout the community. One by one, local leaders took up the challenge to help Kauffman transform Kansas City's formerly erratic baseball fortunes into a stable, hometown effort. Their motivation was a shared love for the game and the chance to earn vacations and trips to Spring Training by selling season tickets. And sell they did. By the fall of 1968, the Lancers had already set a new American League record of 6,441 tickets sold—long before the Royals' first season had even begun.

"Like so many of Kauffman's other ideas, the Lancers were completely unique in sports. Not only did the original members establish the Royals both in the community and at the box office, but they ignited a passion and spearheaded a movement to keep baseball in Kansas City. That original spirit lives on in the Royal Lancers today."

The Lancers are, Nelson summarized, "both a booster club of sorts and a vital part of the organization as a business entity for many years."

For younger fans, the team has Sluggerrrs' Blue Crew, but by the time we checked the site in September 2016, it wasn't possible to determine the price and what was offered in the package—they were sold out. That sort of thing can happen with a World Champion team; the Royals had won the 2015 World Series.

The team offers an annual Fan Fest, maintains a Social Media Clubhouse, a number of other ways in which fans can interact with the team, but other than the very effective Lancers (which was brought in-house within the last 10 years) appears to have no organized fan or booster clubs. There are, of course, online sites for fans such as www.royalsblue.com.

Thanks to Curt Nelson.

Los Angeles Dodgers

The Los Angeles Dodgers have two clubs to note:

The L.A. Dodgers Booster Club describes itself as "a support organization dedicated to bringing the sport of Baseball to the attention of sports lovers the world over, stimulating interest in the Los Angeles Dodgers, providing information that is relative to the sport of Baseball, raising funds to help support financially strapped local Little League Teams, and making our youth more aware of this inspirational pastime."

The club meets on the second Monday of each month, and it publishes *Booster Bits*, a monthly publication for members. A perusal of the publication online at www.dodgersboosterclub.com shows this to be an exceptionally active club.

There is a standard annual adult membership fee of $30.00. Members receive a discount of tickets of "up to 30% off." There have been group trips to various major and minor-league ballparks, as well as to other locations — even China.

Their site says, "Boosters meet and greet Dodgers of the future, help local Little Leagues, and other deserving charitable groups. Boosters enjoy informational and fun monthly meetings, and Meet Ups, participate in annual holiday parties & picnics, ice cream socials, pot luck dinners, Rose Parade Float decorating, Blood Drives, and much more!"

There is also the Go Go Dodgers Fan Club, founded in August 1966. When the Brooklyn Dodgers relocated to L. A. in 1958, there was a Dodger Ball Club (which included members of the Hollywood Stars Fan Club). Go Go Dodgers formed out of there, with 10 members led by first president Yvonne Walters. Initial dues were $5 for area residents and the first monthly meetings were in members' homes.

The fan club soon began to organize road trips to San Francisco beginning in 1971, San Diego starting in 1975, and to Las Vegas at spring training time starting in 1978. In more recent years, club members have attended games of the Rancho Cucamonga Quake minor-league team.

Luncheons were held at Los Angeles hotels, and awards were presented to honor the team's MVP, top rookie, pitcher of the year, and the player who best exemplified Dodger tradition. Among the personalities honored over the years at club events have been Dusty Baker, Steve Garvey, Kirk Gibson, Adrian Gonzalez, Mickey Hatcher, Tommy John, Clayton Kershaw, Tommy Lasorda, Manny Mota, Chan Ho Park, Manny Ramirez, Jerry Reuss, Steve Sax, Mike Scioscia, Reggie Smith, Don Sutton, Fernando Valenzuela, Bob Welch, Maury Wills, and many, many more.

Charitable work has always been important, with a number of organizations benefitting from club efforts, such as sponsoring children from the Inner City Mission and the Rosemead Boys and Girls Club.

Club members also attended the Baseball Writers Association dinner, with picnics, brunches, and the like. As with many organizations of its type, the club membership has tended to decline over the years, to a low of 34 devoted members in 2015. Membership dues for current members at $25 and new members $35. New members receive a fan club shirt with their membership.

It maintains a presence on Facebook at:

https://www.facebook.com/GoGo-Dodgers-Fan-Club-315748381800149/about/?entry_point=page_nav_about_item &tab=page_info

They declare that Go Go Dodgers is "one of the oldest Los Angeles Dodger Fan Clubs." Membership includes discounted rates for tickets to at least 20 games per season, and the opportunity to buy tickets to playoff and World Series games.

We get to throw out the ceremonial 1st pitch at a game each year as well as present awards to the outstanding Dodger players from the prior season.

As a member of the club you will be able to attend playoff & World Series games when the Dodgers are playing

Oddly, there is also a GoGoDodgers Fan Club on Facebook public group, at this address:

https://www.facebook.com/groups/376461315752971/members/

It only lists 11 members, four of whom are named Shaw.

Thanks to Andy McCue, and to Bob Doxey, the Club Historian of GoGoDodgers.

Florida Marlins

The Marlins have organized their own fan club, the Fish Family. What is the Fish Family? From the site: "Being in the Fish Family means rooting the Marlins on through thick and thin. It's for those who remember Charlie Hough's first pitch, Renteria's game-winner, Beckett's shutout and José's rookie season. It's for those who care about the power of our collective spirit - as Marlins fans.

"It's not for everyone - and that's okay. From the players to the coaches, the broadcasters and the fans, we're all in this together. Your support is directly connected to the team's success - and we thank you! You're a Marlins fan." The club has its own loyalty program, where fans can earn points and use them for various purposes. See: https://secure.mlb.com/mia/fan_forum/fanclub.jsp

There is also the Billy's Bunch Kids Club for kids 12 and under. It can be found at: http://miami.marlins.mlb.com/mia/fan_forum/billys-bunch/

Milwaukee Brewers

The Milwaukee Brewers have Brewers Kids, in line with most major-league clubs who offer similar fare. They also have encouraged, in what appears to be a fledgling effort co-sponsored by Southwest Airlines, fans outside Milwaukee from posting their location to a map on the team website as members of Brewers Road Crew. There are a few dozen photographs of Road Crew members at locations around the USA and Canada, in Europe, in Africa, in Australia, hiking the Inca Trail, in front of the Taj Mahal, in the Himalayas, on the Great Wall of China, and even at exotic Fenway Park in Boston. Southwest offered a grand prize to fly two to Denver for the final road trip of the 2016 season against the Colorado Rockies.

Brewer Kids is also a team-organized effort, for kids 14 and under. It costs $25 to join ("a $120 value"), and indeed it does offer good value.

There are six ticket vouchers (must be accompanied by someone 18 or older, such as a parent), a free Brewers Kids Club cap, an ID with lanyard, a drawstring bad, a water bottle, wristbands, and even a Racing Sausage Poster. There's a voucher for a ballpark tour and invites to special events such as Party with the Mascots Day, which was held on June 26 and an on-field parade on the July 31 Kids Club Day. Game tickets were required for participation, but the ticket vouchers did apply on these days.

There is (or was) a start at an organic group, www.brewerfan.net, begun in the year 2001 by Brian Kapellusch. He inspired a lead group of six others, who joined the site over the years and into both 2006 and 2007. It's an ambitious site, prepared to provide a great deal of detail, and it attracted some praise from outside sources. Jim Callis of *Baseball America* dubbed it "an unbelievable site" and Baseball Prospectus in 2005 wrote that it was "indispensable... one of the best team-specific references on the web." But in the fall of 2016, there appears to be little or no recent activity on the site and inquiries sent to the email addresses on the site either bounce back or elicit no response.

Minnesota Twins

Longtime SABR member (and 2016 honoree recipient of the Bob Davids Award) Stew Thornley responded to an inquiry: "I'm not aware of any team fan clubs for the Twins. There were a couple notable ones for players when the Twins were at Met Stadium - Phil Roof and Mike Cubbage. I was in the latter, and we were drunk a lot." Stew has arguably matured over the years and currently serves as official scorer for many Twins games, and other professional sports teams in the Minneapolis-St. Paul area.

The Minnesota Twins team does have its own kids club, Twins Club, run by the team. It is at:

http://minnesota.twins.mlb.com/min/fan_forum/kids_index.jsp

Thanks to Stew Thornley.

New York Mets

Author Matt Silverman answered a request for information: "There is a Mets Booster Club in Port St. Lucie. The person I recall who was in charge was Jim Frietas. Looking them up online finds info on accountants or other stuff that has nothing to do with baseball. The group is active, though, especially in spring training.

"The Mets have a Welcome Home Dinner after Opening Day, but it seems to be done by the team a corporate sponsor and the team. Though I am not even sure of that since the Mets haven't had a winter carnival or Fan Fest for years. The Queens baseball Convention is run by a non-affiliated website, the Mets Police.

"There is a group that has outings all over the country that started as a T-shirt company: the 7 Line Army. It is run by Darren Meehan. It has a permanent presence at Citi Field."

"Fast forward a few years and a new concept was added to our brand, The 7 Line Army. We sit together at games at least once a month at home and on the road. Thousands of die hard fans cheering on our favorite team. Our 'Army' is without a doubt the largest traveling group of supporters in all of baseball."

In 2013 the Army organized six outings. Four at Citi Field, one at Wrigley and one at Yankee Stadium, the first "Bronx Invasion."

In 2014, there were 11 outings. Seven at Citi Field and away trips to SF, Miami, Philly and Yankee Stadium. At this time The 7 Line became an officially licensed MLB brand with a kiosk inside Citi Field.

In 2015, 14 outings were held - nine at Citi Field and away trips to Yankee Stadium, Pittsburgh, Atlanta, Baltimore and Denver."

For 2016 plans included invading KC, SD, MIL, DC and the 4th annual "Bronx Invasion."

See the site at http://the7line.com/pages/about-us

They say, "Win or lose we make our presence known and show the baseball world that Mets fans are up there with the most fun, loyal, dedicated and energetic."

The team does, however, have an official, team-organized "fan club":

http://newyork.mets.mlb.com/nym/fan_forum/club_mets.jsp

It's called Club Mets. Membership includes a pair of complimentary tickets, access opportunities to purchase other tickets, and even one game day complimentary Citi Field scoreboard message!

As with some other team-sponsored clubs, membership closes before the season is over.

Thanks to Matt Silverman.

New York Yankees

The New York Yankees have, for decades, had a large and fervent fan base. It just doesn't seem to have been one that gathers in fan clubs. There are the Bleacher Creatures, of course, the denizens of the right-field bleachers best known for the "Roll Call" they run through at the beginning of each game. In the blurb for Filip Bondy's 2005 book *Bleeding Pinstripes: A Season with the Bleacher Creatures of Yankee Stadium*, he called them "this most dedicated tribe of rooters." Writing for the *New York Daily News* in 1996, he had named them "a core group of the most rabid, passionate fans." But other than loyally populating the ballpark, they don't seem to have fan clubs outside the Stadium.

Longtime Yankees fan (and author of *The 50 Greatest Yankees Games*) Cecilia Tan responded to a query regarding Yankees fan or booster clubs: "The only club I know of like that for the Yankees is the Lehigh Valley Yankees Club, which is a group in Pennsylvania. I don't know how to contact them but I hear about them from time to time and I think when *50 Greatest Yankees* came out they got in touch about me doing an interview or something. That might have been the first time I heard of them. I see their name on the scoreboard from time to time."

Michael Margolis, Assistant Director of Media Relations for the Yankees, replied in late August 2016, "Unfortunately, we don't have a list of groups you're asking about on file. Sorry I can't be more help to you on this request."

A websearch reveals that an organization set itself up as "New York Yankees Fan Club," apparently in early 2013, with the address of http://newyorkyankeesfanclub.com. They announced an office on Lexington Avenue, with the grandiose email address of executiveoffices@newyorkyankeesfanclub.com. However, actually clicking on that address re-routed the email address to one tours@newyorkcityonsale.com. The site promises "5,000 Free Home-game, Game-day, Entrance tickets — to anybody who would like to see the Yankees play a home game at Yankee Stadium live," as long as they do not live in the Northeastern United States. They wrote, "If you are interested in visiting New York City, and/or in seeing the Yankees play baseball at Yankee Stadium, contact us here" and then provides a form for prospective visitors to fill out. Underneath a lot of Yankees-oriented material, not updated since prior to the 2013 season, one finds that this is a travel agency hoping to do some business booking Yankees fans into hotel and travel packages. That it hasn't been updated, and still features images of Mariano Rivera, etc. leads one to guess that perhaps the venture wasn't as successful as the planners had hoped.

The team itself offers a number of clubs more or less following the template one finds on other MBL team sites. See http://newyork.yankees.mlb.com/nyy/fan_forum/universe.jsp. Clearly, they wanted to "one-up" Red Sox Nation, by naming themselves something grander: Yankees Universe. Several different packages may be seen, including tickets, discounts, t-shirts, and even a "Yankees Stress Ball" (which has perhaps become more useful in the years since 2009.) In addition to three standard packages, there is also a Golf Package including 50 tees and a sleeve of three golf balls, a Baby Package with two baby bottles and two pacifiers (we can leave out the too-obvious joke), and even a Puppy Package with a certificate, a dog lead, a dog charm, and "Access to members-only website with exclusive content and offers for puppy parents." The Puppy Package only costs $35.95 per year.

This offer is valid to anyone who does not reside in the North-Eastern United States—and includes our fans from other countries—especially those countries from which we have players on the New York Yankees roster—Panama (Mariano Rivera), Dominican Republic (Robinson Cano), Japan (Hiroki Kuroda and Ichiro Suzuki).

Thanks to Michael Margolis and Cecilia Tan.

Oakland Athletics

Membership in the Oakland Athletics Booster Club "includes newsletters, notices of special events, your participation at our monthly booster luncheons, tailgates during the season as well as group tickets to certain games throughout the baseball season." Membership costs $25.00 per year. Cost for the luncheons at the West Side Club is $21 for cash/check, or $22 for payment via credit card or PayPal.

The club's website further explains its mission: "The Oakland Athletics Booster Club is an organization of fans dedicated to supporting and promoting the Oakland Athletics baseball team, with a mission of raising funds to support charities associated with the Oakland Athletics Community Fund. Group game tickets and parking passes for selected games during the regular season in Oakland and spring training at home games in Mesa are available for Booster Club members. Periodic pregame tailgates are held in the Coliseum parking lot during the season. Members receive a monthly newsletter. The Booster Club has a monthly luncheon during the baseball season in the West Side Club at the Oakland Coliseum. The luncheon program includes a guest speaker associated with the A's organization." See http://www.oaklandathleticsboosterclub.com/

Money raised by the club benefits the Bill King Scholarship Fund, part of the Oakland A's Community Fund, a 501(C)(3) charitable organization. The Bill King Fund provides scholarship assistance for college students majoring in broadcast journalism.

There is a team-organized A's Kids Club, for $15 plus $5 handling. The membership kit includes a beanie, a drawstring bag, tattoo sleeves, and a lanyard, as well as coupons for discounts on A's tickets and merchandise—and discounts at Round Table Pizza and the Oakland Zoo. Members also get a Kids Club Passport that can be stamped at games and earn one certain prizes. For those who aren't ready to spring for the package, a Kids Club Rookie membership is available for free. For more information on the A's Kids Club: http://oakland.athletics.mlb.com/oak/fan_forum/kids/kids-club/

There is one more group worthy of mention here: the Oakland A's Fan Coalition. It was a fan group formed in 1998, and formed for a purpose, reminiscent in its way of the Save Fenway Park! group, which in Boston helped successfully fight the attempt to replace Fenway Park. Lilian Bartholo explains in a September 24, 2016 email that it is a closed Facebook group maintained as "an informational and a watchdog group…as a testament of efforts we made back when the Haas ownership sold the team in 1995. As we watched the new owners of the A's take over the franchise we noticed they were trying to relocate the A's out of Oakland." The OAFC's purpose is to preserve and honor the legacy of Oakland A's baseball." See the group at: Our OAFC group exists since 1998 and our goal has been to preserve and honor the legacy of Oakland A's baseball. We support keeping the A's in Oakland and we are strongly against relocation of our team outside of Oakland where they belong. Our OAFC group exists since 1998 and our goal has been to preserve and honor the legacy of Oakland A's baseball. We support keeping the A's in Oakland and we are strongly against relocation of our team outside of Oakland where they belong. Our OAFC group exists since 1998 and our goal has been to preserve and honor the legacy of Oakland A's baseball. We support keeping the A's in Oakland and we are strongly against relocation of our team outside of Oakland where they belong.

https://www.facebook.com/groups/oafctalk/. Lil Bartholo mentions another allied group, BaseballOakland.com, similarly determined to pressure the team's current owners to make improvements at the Coliseum, but also to embrace Oakland and its tradition of baseball.

Thanks to Lilian Bartholo and Marlene Vogelsang.

Philadelphia Phillies

The Fightin' Phils Fan Club is a team-organized group, with an annual membership fee of $24.99. The most attractive element is the pair of complimentary tickets to a Phillies home game. One also gets discounts to the team store, online or at the park. There are also opportunities to buy tickets on presale, and acquire access to early batting practice, and the opportunity to purchase tickets to Fightin' Phils Fan Club bus trip to an away game. See http://philadelphia. phillies.mlb.com/phi/fan_forum/fightin_phils.jsp

There is also Phillies Kids, for Phanatic phans under 14. It's at: http://philadelphia.phillies.mlb.com/phi/fan_forum/kids_index.jsp

The kids club has a $13 membership package which gets you a lunch bag, a sandwich holder, a poster, a birthday card, and a few other things.

Alternatively, there is a $15 Junior Phillies Club, "presented by Powerade," which includes a Phillies backpack, a wristband, two vouchers for tickets to a Junior Phillies Club Night in September, a newsletter and emails, and "first in line" privileges at Kids Run the Bases events.

There's even a Phillies Newborn Club. That one costs $40, and gets you a personalized Phillies birth certificate (whether this might help later if voter ID laws are tightened is yet to be determined), a PhanaVision photo birth announcement (your baby's picture on the electronic scoreboard), a Rookie of the Year bib, a pair of pre-walker sneakers in Phils red and white, a birthday card at the first birthday, and a "special ticket offer to bring the little one to his/her first Phillies game." And more.

Pittsburgh Pirates

For kids, there is the Bucaroos Fan Club at http://pittsburgh.pirates.mlb.com/pit/fan_forum/kidsclub.jsp

There's a free Silver Membership and a $30 Premium Gold Membership. Both include free Pirates tickets and free Chick-fil-A® offers. So why might you want the Gold one? Well, you get a

Welcome Letter from the Pirate Parrot, a BKC Membership Badge, batting practice viewings on participating dates, four (4) free Pirates ticket vouchers (redeemable at the Pirates Box Office only), six (6) BOGO ticket vouchers (Redeemable Online or at the Pirates Box Office), three free Chick-fil-A® offers, one BKC cinch bag, and a pair of BKC sunglasses. Not only that, but "There are more great prizes and experiences available with the more games you attend." In case you were wondering, BOGO means Buy One, Get One—in other words, on top of the four vouchers, you can get six more free tickets if you buy six accompanying tickets. Needless to say, there are certain restrictions that apply. You also get free emails. With the Silver membership, you get one free ticket voucher (pretty good, because you're getting a free ticket with a free membership), one Chick-fil-A coupon, and four BOGO vouchers.

Non-kids seem to be out of luck as far as fan clubs go. On Facebook, though, there is the Pittsburgh Pirates Raise the Jolly Roger Fan Club, of Ford City, PA. And the usual commercial sites such as www.bucsdugout.com and http://fansided.com/mlb/mlb-teams/pittsburgh-pirates.

St. Louis Cardinals

Ron Watermon, Vice-President of Communications for the St. Louis Cardinals wrote on August 26, 2016, "I'm not familiar with any organized groups, but will forward the inquiry to a few others to see if they know of any." Presumably he was referring only to so-called "organic" fan clubs or booster clubs, because the Cardinals do run their own fan club, Redbird Nation.

It's at http://stlouis.cardinals.mlb.com/stl/fan_forum/redbird_nation.jsp

For a $19.95 annual membership, in 2016, one gets a discount to team store wares, MLB Gameday audio, buy one-get-one-free tickets to a ballpark tour, and—most attractively—two tickets to a regular season 2016 Cardinals home game (via voucher code to be redeemed online for select Monday-Thursday games only.) Offers like that clearly make it worth the price of membership. Members do get other things of less-certain value, such as "Special Access to Redbird Nation members-only pages." But it's hard to cavil at such curiosities, when one can get two game tickets for $19.95.

It's no surprise that there is also Cardinals Kids. Oddly, though, it costs just over $10.00 more — membership is $30.00. It's for kids under 14 years old. Their site is: http://stlouis.cardinals.mlb.com/stl/fan_forum/kids_index.jsp

There is, additionally, the Cardinals Varsity Club (presented by Rawlings) for youngsters 14-18. This one is the most expensive package — $35.00. But both youth-oriented memberships also get you two free tickets, and a t-shirt, and quite a bit more — a free hot dog/soda coupon, a free visit to the batting cage and "fast-pitch" machine at the park, and other coupons for the official scorecard, two game day magazines, and a free stadium tour. Regardless of the level, these are undeniably very good deals. The pricing for the various levels is kind of quirky, though.

St. Louis Cardinals Social Club

It is sometimes the case that a ballclub may have fan clubs without realizing it. This may more often be the case if the club is situated fairly far from the team's home park. The St. Louis Cardinals Social Club is based in the Chapel Hill, North Carolina area and has attracted 35-40 members to each of its annual gatherings. The club began in February 2012 when Joe Vanderford, a Cardinals fan and ESPN cameraman, and Paul Gardner were talking about how many Cardinals fans they knew in the area. "Joe suggested that we try to get everyone together somehow," Paul said, "so we started talking with my dad Randy and a couple others about ways we might schedule a gathering. We have about 50 people on our mailing list. The list grows each year as we add friends of those in attendance or meet new Cards fans (saw a guy in a Cards cap at my son's baseball game last spring, for instance, so we've added him to the list).

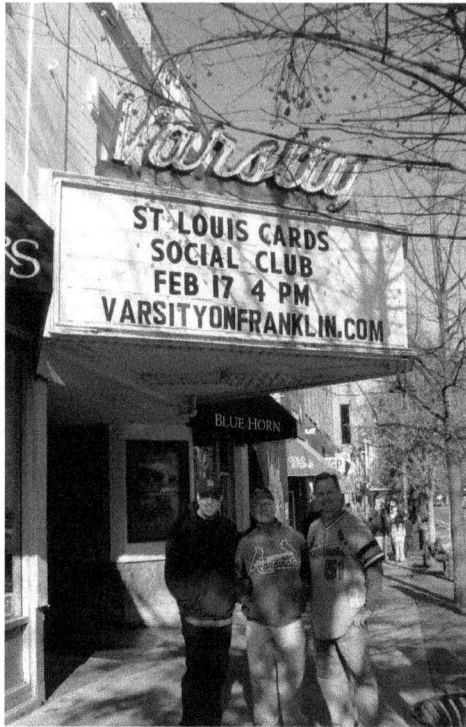

*St. Louis Cardinals Social Club: Joe
Vanderford, Randy Gardner, Paul Gardner
before their first gathering on February 17, 2012.*

"Most folks are in the Chapel Hill area, but we have a few people come in from Greensboro, a father and son from Virginia, and a friend we met through a Cardinals listserv came in from Indianapolis one year.

"The first year we met we gathered at a movie theater, had popcorn, peanuts, Cracker Jack, and beverages. We watched the official 2011 World Series highlights DVD on the big screen and all stood and cheered when Freese hit his triple and homer in Game Six. Another year, we gathered at a sports bar and, while we had 1964 and 1967 World Series highlights running, most people ate and circulated among tables meeting and talking about the Cardinals, baseball in general, etc. Last year, we were fortunate to have Gary LaRocque, from the Cardinals front office, join us and talk about the

Cardinals farm system. We usually have door prizes through a drawing—Cardinals books, other baseball-related materials we collect throughout the year. We've talked about getting together to watch a game during the regular season or playoffs, but we haven't pulled that off yet." When writing this in late September 2016, Paul added, "A friend said we're going to change the name to St. Louis Gripe Club this year."

Thanks to Ron Watermon, and to Paul and Randy Gardner.

San Diego Padres

The longest-lasting "organic" fan group—the San Diego Madres, a charitable not-for-profit organization founded back in 1972. They are "an organization of women and men who love baseball and their community. The mission of the San Diego Madres is to provide all children in San Diego County with the opportunity to play baseball and softball by providing financial assistance to deserving leagues."

The Madres hold luncheons and dinners, spring training trips, and road trips, as well as luaus and harbor cruises. They are very active in supporting community organizations. Today the Madres provide annual support to, among their beneficiaries, more than 50 leagues representing more than 500 teams.

The San Diego Compadres is the "official fan loyalty program of the San Diego Padres." It's free for all fans, though season ticketholders are automatically enrolled. Fans can accumulate points and use them for auction items and "Marketplace items." When it was kicked off, the Compadres attracted a membership as high as 140,000 fans.

Compadres Kids is for fans 14 years of age and younger. They have the typical "Kids Run the Bases."

San Francisco Giants

A couple of referrals led me to someone said to be likely to know. I got back the following response:

I am not aware of any Fan Club for the San Francisco Giant's (sic). There are fans everywhere.

Good luck with your project.

In fact, the Giants do have a kids club, organized by the team with the corporate look that characterizes many of these MLB kids club site. It is called Giants Kids and can be found at

http://sanfrancisco.giants.mlb.com/sf/fan_forum/kids_index.jsp

The team's website does not indicate any team-organized fan groups, other than the kids club.

Thanks to Marlene Vogelsang and Tom O'Doul.

Seattle Mariners

The RBI Club (Real Baseball Involvement) is a group of longtime season ticketholders who have monthly luncheons during the season, occasional book club events, and an annual dinner and auction that raises funds for Rick's Toys for Kids (http://www.rickstoysforkids. org/), which provides holiday gifts for kids in the greater Seattle community who might not otherwise receive them.

Commissioner Bob Simeone of the RBI Club and Secretary Nancy Abramson provided some background on the organization. Local business executives in the Pacific Northwest created the club under the direction of the Seattle Mariners Baseball Club. It began when the franchise was about four years old in 1980.

The club's history, available on its website (http://marinersrbi-club.com/) explains that it was formed after the 1979 All-Star game in Seattle. It was originally patterned after the Royal Lancers, a volunteer sales group for the Kansas City Royals. The original six owners enthusiastically supported the program. Club founders included: Jay Porter, president of Unigard Insurance Co., serving as Commissioner; Virgil Fassio, publisher of the *Seattle Post-Intelligencer*, serving as League Co-President; and the late Andy Smith, president of Pacific Northwest Bell, serving as League Co-President.

Among the club's historical achievements was our participation in the 1995 campaign to build a new baseball stadium in Seattle.

In the 80s and the 90s the club was dedicated to helping the Mariners sell additional season tickets to local companies in the Pacific

Northwest. With the professionalization of Sports Administration those tasks have migrated to the paid full time staff of the Mariners. The focus of the club is now as a fan club and a way to support the players, coaches, broadcasters, and other Mariners employees in their respective charitable endeavors.

Being a season ticket holder qualifies you for membership. But, Bob explained, "We are also open to dedicated fans recommended by Season Ticket Holders, and Prospective full or fractional Season Ticket Holders suggested for membership by the Mariners. We hold about seven lunches on various Fridays during the baseball season on a monthly basis. We also have one to four offseason events. Those include charitable events, book signings by authors or baseball related books, meetings with coaches or umpires, etc."

"The Mariners are an invaluable resource to the club for Programs and Speakers. However, we are financially independent of the Mariners, and have about 15% -25% of our events away from Safeco Field."

Lunches range from 60 to 120 attendees. Most are in the 75 to 95 range.

Our trip to Cooperstown to see Griffey inducted was 52, our recent trip to see the AquaSox the Mariners short season squad was 40. We tend to have about 10-20 at the Rick Rizzs Toys for Kids Gala, and event with about 350 attendees.

Examples of other events follow:

Book signing and discussion with authors:

Jamie Moyer, "Just tell me I can't"

Michael Tackett, "The Baseball Whisperer."

Larry Colton, "The Southern League."

Lucas Mann, "Class A."

Media Day with representatives from print journalism, web based journalism, radio, t.v. etc. giving their off season perspective on the upcoming year of play.

Alumni Days: Former players, wives, broadcasters reflecting on their times in baseball. Past guests have included Mel Stottlemyre,

Ray Washburn, your own Mr. Castiglione, Mrs. Niehaus, Edgar Martinez, etc.

Nancy Abramson adds: "Included in our monthly luncheons we hold a raffle, and/or an auction with a basket of goodies, baseball tickets, or sometimes a trip and tour to another ball park for a game. The money raised goes to one of our designated charities. Sometimes it goes to the charity of choice of our featured speaker. We have raised money for Angelman's Syndrome, The Martinez Foundation, Toys for Kids, Umpires Care and Mariners Care. Our members like having this component to their membership.

"Every other year we hold a Members Business meeting with wine, beer and appetizers, where members can come with questions they may have about the workings and programs of RBI. It is a great opportunity for members to make suggestions and critiques of the program.

"One of our most popular programs is with the umpires. We have had one or more for the last few years and it is fun to get their perspective on the game and how they see their roles. The Q & A is always interesting. In addition we have the "Young Guns" in September with the final call ups in place and they are always entertaining. The other months are coaches, players, members of the media, perhaps a visiting broadcaster from another team, sometimes the GM or executive in the Mariners organization. Our members seem to like the variety.

"RBI has also had tables at various luncheons both at Safeco Field and off site. We have a strong presence at the annual Toys for Kids auction, The Martinez Foundation luncheon, and lunches where former Mariners have been honored. We also just hosted a luncheon at a popular waterfront restaurant featuring Bret Boone discussing his book and being interviewed by a local sports reporter."

Thanks to Bob Simeone and Nancy Abramson.

Tampa Bay Rays

The Rays have a fairly active fan group on Facebook, with 380 "members," at https://www.facebook.com/groups/TBRaysFanClub/

For the most part, though, they seem to rely on setting up their own fan clubs. They don't have one for grownups, but they do have a Social Media page on their website where they try to attract and encourage fans to communicate via Twitter and Snapchat. And for those fans who may be seeking love on the Tampa Bay Rays site, they have Rays Singles—which turns out to be a portal for Match. com—"Find other Single Rays Fans."

Rays Kids and Rays Rookies both take you to the same place: http://tampabay.rays.mlb.com/tb/fan_forum/rays_rookies.jsp, though (in contrast to the practice of most other teams), there is no club for kids to join. There is a lot of information about Raymond, the team mascot, and a number of activities such as an online coloring book and quizzes, videos, and more.

Texas Rangers

Mona Neill detailed the history of The Texas Rangers Women's Club (TRWC), which was organized in August of 1974, with the assistance of Phil Jason, a member of the Texas Rangers baseball club.

"The Rangers sponsored a picnic with the manager Billy Martin and the players in July 1974 for any woman interested in the organization. The charter meeting was held in October 1974 with the officers being elected, the bylaws were drawn, and the TRWC was born.

"Per our By Laws: The Texas Rangers Women's Club is an independent volunteer organization, which promotes fellowship among its members, generating enthusiasm for the Texas Rangers Baseball Club, enabling less fortunate citizens to enjoy baseball through funds raised by Ways and Means projects, and working promotions for the Texas Rangers Baseball Club. The Texas Rangers Women's Club provides volunteer services to the Texas Rangers Baseball Club, at the baseball club's direction and discretion.

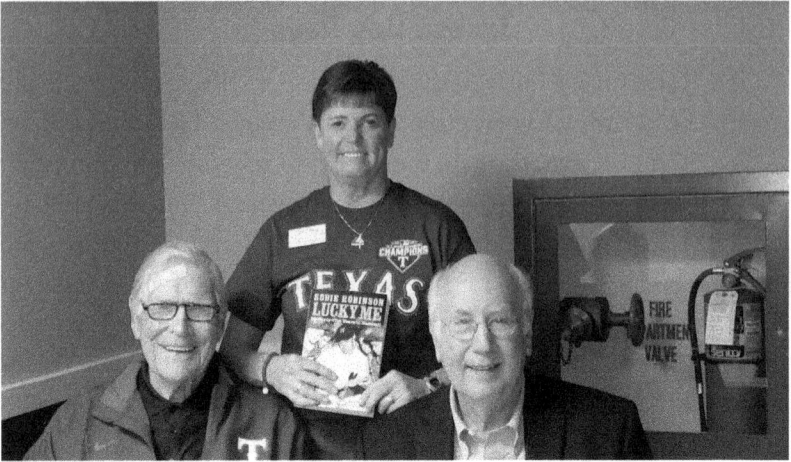

Mona Neill of the Texas Rangers Women's Fan Club between Eddie Robinson and Paul Rogers.

"Our main job is to help the Rangers Promotions staff hand out the promotion items at the gates such as bobble heads, T shirts, hats, etc., but we also help host less fortunate groups to a Ranger game each month. The Rangers provide the tickets and we help assist them to their seats, provide hot dogs, drinks and snacks, and visit with them during the games. In addition we do community outreach such as working at food banks, adopt a highway program, donate back to school supplies, and donate to designated charities. Of course we are not 'just about work'. We have monthly meetings but also social outings to ball games, plays, picnics, theaters, and restaurants.

"This is our 42nd year and we still have three women active in the club ("Charter" members) that have been with the club from the beginning. I have attached a photo of them receiving their charter member awards at our 2014 banquet. We try to get occasional guest speaker/s for our monthly meetings. I have also attached a photo from last Nov. of me with a couple of speakers you may recognize :o) Besides volunteering for the Rangers, some of our ladies do occasional volunteer work at the National Cowgirl Hall of Fame and Museum. (Our former Rangers promotions boss is the Membership Director over there and her mom is a member of our club :o) A handful of our ladies also give out promotion items for our local hockey team, the Dallas Stars, but get paid for this.

"We have approximately 200 members, over the last three to four years. Membership skyrocketed after 2010 and 2011 because of being in the World Series.

"Our membership fee is $25 per year, plus a one-time $7 fee for a name tag. The money is used for copies, postage, etc.

"Hopefully this gives you some idea about our club. We have a Facebook page that has lots of pictures and should provide additional information as well."

The club's Facebook page may be found at:

https://www.facebook.com/Texas-Rangers-Womens-Club-145792845453789/?fref=ts

Thanks to John Blake, Mona Neill, C. Paul Rogers, and Steve West.

Toronto Blue Jays

Invited to explain a bit about the history of the Toronto Blue Jays Fan Club, Sue Ross, who was the club's web operator, explained that the first person to start the fan club was Harvey Trivett. When he died, Jean Douglas took over the club but running the club perhaps was too much for her. An appeal was issued seeking people who might have interest in running a Blue Jays Fan Club and requesting they submit a letter saying why they loved the Jays or why the Jays should have a fan club.

She says, "I was one of the chosen and we had about 10 board members. Our activities included road trips, lunches, batting practice visits, and player interviews. It was all a lot of fun. I think we had about 1,700 members and this included members from the USA and abroad."

For about 10 years, starting in 1998, the club also published *Full Count*, which included interviews with players and other team personnel. It was distributed to those fans all over Canada, the United States, and internationally who had signed up for the fan club.

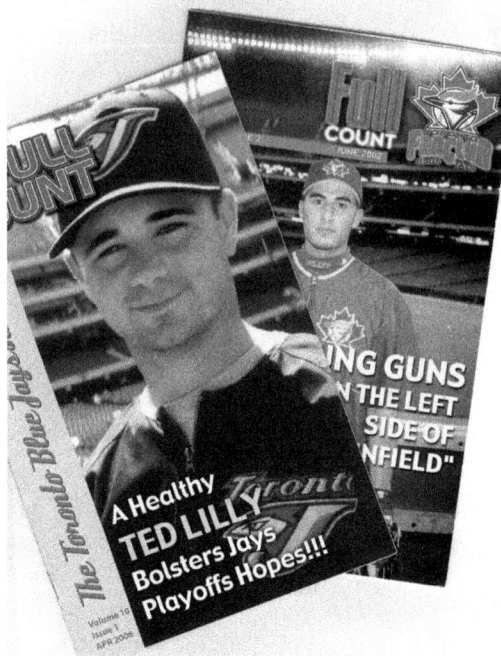

Toronto Blue Jays Fan Club publications.

In time, the club was discontinued. Some board members were moving away, one had health problems, and the ones who remained were ones who had fulltime jobs and could not commit enough time to the Fan Club.

The Blue Jays themselves took over the fan club, but within a year or two folded it. The ballclub still runs a Junior Jays program for younger fans.

Thanks to John Matthew and Susan Ross.

Washington Nationals

The Half-Street Irregulars (HSI) is an invitation-only Washington Nationals fan group that believes in sharing a positive baseball experience, having fun, and giving back. Our group's name is a play on the Baker Street Irregulars, the first Sherlockian society. But in this case,

Half Street ends at the center-field gate of Nationals Park and we are the first organized fan club of the Washington Nationals.

HSI was founded in February 2013 by Frank Lattuca (@Nationals101) and a group of committed fans who all met on Twitter. We realized, in the wake of the Nationals' loss in Game Five of the 2012 National League Division Series, that we weren't alone in our mourning. Each of us found solace with other fans on Twitter, which led to a few in person meetings where we mourned. But in those meetings we also went over all the great moments of the season, which was the first winning one for the Nationals. At one of those get-togethers, Frank suggested the idea of an organized fan group and HSI was born. After four seasons, we've grown from about 30 committed fans to almost 100.

We are always on the look-out for good fans, both at Nats Park and on Twitter. But there is no formula for becoming a member. If someone is interested in joining HSI, we suggest they come to our events and/or get to know our members on Twitter. That way we can get to know them and they can get to know us. Most of our events are open to the public and are advertised through our Twitter account, @Half_St_Irr.

HSI is not affiliated with the Washington Nationals, staff, players, families, or members of the media. But given our fun and positive approach to fandom, we've been able to work with individual players and/or their wives to put on player tributes that sometimes also serve as charitable fundraisers. In 2015, we partnered with the Denard Span Foundation for the #HashtagSpanning party, with Ian Desmond for #DesiNight to support the Central Union Mission Food Bank, with Ashley Fister to support the Washington Humane Society through our #DougAndMrHiss event (Doug Fister's cat is named Mr. Hiss), and with the ZiMS Foundation for #EotRSB2 (our 2nd End of the Regular Season Blowout). In 2016, we raised money at #EspiBeardDay for Danny Espinosa's favorite charity, Project Access, and the #RedPorchStampede was a tribute to the Buffalo, Wilson Ramos, that raised money for feeding people in his native Venezuela.

All of these events took place at the Red Porch, our self-proclaimed home inside Nationals Park. As the 2016 season draws to a close, we're raising money for the Nationals Youth Baseball Academy through two events — a Field Day at the Academy and #EotRSB3 at Nationals Park.

In addition to our player tributes, we sponsor watch parties for #Clinchmas (when the Nats might clinch a postseason berth), the annual #HSIUNFAP (HSI Unofficial NatsFest After Party), and our first (but not last) road trip, #HSIatCITI. For the latter, we got around 125 Nats fans together, put some of them on a charter bus, and went up to Citi Field over Labor Day weekend 2016. We've also done some really silly things like organized an "O Canada" national anthem sing-a-long when the Toronto Blue Jays were in town, to pay tribute to our franchise's northern roots. We also sponsored an oven mitt night in 2014 when both Ryan Zimmerman and Bryce Harper were sporting mitts, when running the bases, to protect their still healing broken fingers. Whether silly or raising serious money, HSI is all about having fun and supporting our team! And in case you're wondering, we are adamantly against the wave. #KillTheWave

Note: The team›s High-A affiliate has its own support group, the Potomac Nationals Booster Club. Several members of the Half Street Irregulars are active with the PNats Booster Club, as well. The Potomac Nationals Boosters Club is a venerable one, which has seen it associated with six different franchises over the years, under changing names. Lamar Boone of the Club reports in February 5, 2017 email: "Our Booster Club's origin was with the Alexandria Dukes in the 70's. It continued with the franchise move to Prince William County in 1984 and has supported High A teams affiliated with the Pirates ('84-'87), Yankees ('88-'93), White Sox ('94-'96), Cardinals ('97-2002), Reds ('03-'04) and Nationals (2005-). Our membership base average over the past 10 years is 75 families."

Thanks to Frank Lattuca, Lisa Rodely, and Jen Underwood of the Irregulars, Amanda Comak of the Washington Nationals, Lamar Boone of the Potomac National Booster Club, and David Vincent.

Fan Clubs – A New Commercial Enterprise

There is also a business which makes up fan clubs for various teams, presumably as a way of making money, cashing in on the fan bases of the various teams.

http://fansided.com/network/mlb/

The Red Sox "club" run by FanSided is called BoSox Injection. It doesn't really purport to be a fan club, but proclaims itself as "the Boston Red Sox news and opinions site brought to you by the FanSided Network. BoSox Injection is dedicated to providing top-notch Red Sox news, views. and original content. This site also serves as a community for like-minded fans to come together to catch up on the latest news and to discuss their passion."

About FanSided:

The idea of FanSided was born in 2007, when two brothers felt that their favorite team, the Kansas City Chiefs, was being under-covered by the mainstream media. Taking matters into their own hands, they launched Arrowhead Addict, a move that would spawn the creation of FanSided in 2009, a network of over 300+ fan-powered unique sports, entertainment and lifestyle sites dedicated to team-specific, sport-specific, genre-specific, and fanbase-specific coverage.

From sports, movies and TV to lifestyle and tech, FanSided has you covered.

Fan Clubs For Teams That No Longer Exist

In addition to active fan clubs for today's major-league teams, there are also a number of "fan clubs" for former big-league teams.

Several clubs maintain a presence on Facebook, or elsewhere on the internet. See, for instance:

Boston Braves Historical Association = https://www.facebook.com/BostonBravesHA/

Montreal Expos = http://exposnation.com/en/

New York Giants Preservation Society = https://www.facebook.com/New-York-Giants-Preservation-Society-BASEBALL-160353950762500/

Philadelphia Athletics = http://philadelphiaathletics.org/baseball-history/

St. Louis Browns = https://www.facebook.com/SaintLouisBrowns

Notes

1   NOTE: Edward Hanify has been omitted from this list, though according to the *Boston Herald* of February 16, he was also a legal advisor.

2   Author interview with Ken Coleman, December 17, 2001. Unless otherwise indicated, all quotations from Ken Coleman come from this interview which will be noted as Ken Coleman interview.

3   For a comprehensive book focused on the Red Stockings, see Bob LeMoine and Bill Nowlin, eds., *Boston's First Nine: The 1871-75 Boston Red Stockings* (Phoenix: SABR, 2016).

4   Peter J. Nash, *Boston's Royal Rooters* (Charleston, South Carolina: Arcadia Publishing, 2005).

5   "Northamptons 4, University of Vermonts 3," *Springfield Republican*, July 29, 1891: 5.

6   "The Doom of the 'Colts'," *Boston Daily Advertiser*, June 13, 1892: 4.

7   "The Yale Game," *Boston Journal*, June 24, 1892: 3.

8   "They Played Ball, They Did," *Boston Herald*, July 17, 1892: 17.

9   "'Reds' Beaten," *Boston Journal*, September 19, 1892: 3; "Waning Interest in Baseball," *Springfield Republican*, October 3, 1892: 5; "It Is A Very Close Race," *Boston Herald*, December 5, 1892: 8.

10   "But Four Hits," *Boston Globe*, September 10, 1890: 7.

11   "Making A Baseball," *St. Louis Post-Dispatch*, May 11, 1890: 28.

12   "Playing Worse Than Ever," *Chicago Daily Tribune*, May 24, 1890: 6.

13   'Base-Ball Cranks," *Hartford Courant*, July 8, 1890: 1.

14   Rooters and Rooting," *New York Sun*, re-published in the *Chicago Tribune*, July 6, 1891: 7.

15   "Yes, the Bostons," *Boston Journal*, April 29, 1893: 3.

16   "Dr. Everett A 'Rooter'," *Boston Globe*, May 6, 1894: 9.

17   Joanne Hulbert, "Hi Hi Dixwell," in Bill Nowlin, ed., *New Century, New Team: The 1901 Boston Americans* (Phoenix: SABR, 2013), 178-181.

18   Peter J. Nash, "Mike 'Nuf Ced' McGreevy," Bill Nowlin, ed., *New Century, New Team: The 1901 Boston Americans* (Phoenix: SABR, 2013), 182-198.

19   T. H. Murnane, "In the Stretch," *Boston Globe*, September 13, 1897: 5.

20 "Off to the Scene: Rooters Have Gone with Lungs and Badges," *Boston Globe*, September 24, 1897: 1. The badge was depicted in the page one story.

21 "The Boston-Baltimore Game," *Springfield Republican*, September 27, 1897: 5; "Boston Takes Two in Three in Baltimore," *Boston Daily Advertiser*, September 28, 1897: 1.

22 "On the Baseball Field," *New York Times*, September 29, 1897: 4.

23 "Players' Dinner; 'Loyal Rooters' Gave It At Faneuil Hall," *Boston Globe*, October 7, 1897: 5.

24 Peter J. Nash, "Mike 'Nuf Ced' McGreevy."

25 Peter J. Nash, *Boston's Royal Rooters* (Charleston, South Carolina: Arcadia Publishing, 2005), 7.

26 Harold Kaese, "*The Boston Braves, 1871-1953* (Boston: Northeastern University Press, 2004), 101. The book is a reprint of a 1948 and 1954 publication from G. P. Putnam's Sons.

27 "Sporting Notes," *Worcester Daily Spy*, June 9, 1901: 3.

28 "Rooters Leave Here Sanguine," *Boston Herald*, October 5, 1903: 5. John Dooley was, of course, among them.

29 Roger Abrams, *The First World Series and the Baseball Fanatics of 1903* (Boston: Northeastern University Press, 2003), 117.

30 "To Renew the Struggle," *Boston Globe*, October 12, 1903: 3.

31 Lawrence Ritter, The Glory of Their Times (New York: Harper, 1992), 27. A thorough look at the "Tessie" phenomenon (including its revival in 2004) is detailed in Chuck Burgess and Bill Nowlin, *Love That Dirty Water: The Standells and the Improbable Red Sox Victory Anthem* (Burlington, Massachusetts: Rounder Books, 2007.)

32 "Elizabeth Dooley; Devoted Red Sox Fan Attended More Than 4,000 Games," *Los Angeles Times*, July 24, 2000.

33 "Championship Is Landed By Boston Again," *Boston Herald*, October 12, 1904: 4.

34 I. E. Sanborn, "Frown on Rooters Clubs," *Chicago Tribune*, March 8, 1908: B2.

35 The full story of this tour is told in Bill Nowlin, *The Great Red Sox Spring Training Tour of 1911: Sixty-three Games, Coast to Coast* (Jefferson, North Carolina: McFarland & Co., 2010.)

36 Bill Nowlin & Jim Prime, *From The Babe to the Beards: The Boston Red Sox in the World Series* (New York: Sports Publishing, 2014), 32-33.

37 Ibid., 39.

38 "Loyal Royal Rooters Will Leave Today," *Boston Globe*, October 7, 1915: 9.

39 Lawrence J. Sweeney, "New York Greets the Royal Rooters," *Boston Globe*, October 10, 1916: 6.

40 John J. Hallahan, "Gov. M'Call Is Ruth Admirer," *Boston Herald*, September 10, 1918: 4.

41 The *Boston Globe* wrote, "The disagreement and the National Commission and the contesting players, which held up the starting of Tuesday's game, was the thing that kept the public away yesterday." See Edward F. Martin, "Red Sox Win Sixth Game and the Title," *Boston Globe*, September 12, 1918: 1.

42 Bob Ryan, "You Can't Judge It One Game At A Time," *Boston Globe*, August 30, 2009: D1.

43 A nice portrait of Dooley was offered by Huck Finnegan, "Over the Years with Jack Dooley," *Boston Record American*, September 20, 1963: 31.

44 "Rooters Glorify the Achievements of Red Sox," *Boston Journal*, January 31, 1913: 10.

45 This section on the Winter League, as well as the section on John S. Dooley which follows both come from Bill Nowlin, *Red Sox Threads* (Burlington, Massachusetts: Rounder Books, 2008).

46 Handwritten notes for a speech found in Katherine Dooley's papers.

47 "Mike Ryba Feted by Bull Pen A.C., Gets $1000 Gift," *Boston Globe*, September 23, 1945: D31.

48 Harold Kaese, "Ryba Gave His All Until the End," *Boston Globe*, December 15, 1971: 51.

49 Harold Kaese, "Dom Leads Off for BoSox Club," *Boston Globe*, February 16, 1967: 49.

50 Alan Frazer, "My Boston," *Boston American*, May 25, 1953: 25.

51 *Boston Daily Record*, November 29, 1954: 55.

52 Harold Kaese, "Concannon Hub of B. C. Attack," *Boston Globe*, September 20, 1963: 37. Huck Finnegan, *op.cit.*, had noted that Dooley was "actually eligible for a Three-Quarter Century medallion."

53 Clif Keane, "Duffy Lewis Feted at Fenway," *Boston Globe*, September 18, 1966: 59.

54 Roger Birtwell, "Wenz and Lahoud, 8 Other Sox Cut," *Boston Globe*, March 22, 1968: 27.

55 John Gillooly, "Belated Salute to Ex-Bruin Flaman," *Boston Record American*, February 25, 1967: 30.

56 Bob Brady, email to author, July 17, 2016. Bob explained that the Quinn letter appeared in the Spring Training Issue-March, 1947 of the *Braves Bulletin*. Were such clubs formed? Brady continued: Evidence exists of at least one such organization. The July, 1947 *Braves Bulletin* reported the following:

"ASHLAND BOOSTERS FETE PRESIDENT OF BRAVES"

"A home town boy who has achieved success in a number of activities was honored prior to the Braves-Dodgers night game of June 27 when 200 members of the Ashland, Mass. Boosters Club gathered at the Wigwam to let Lou Perini know that they appreciate his kindness to them. In brief, simple pre-game ceremonies Henry J.

Shaughnessy, President of The Ashland Club, presented the Tribal President with a Telechron Clock for his 'sportsmanship and everlasting willingness to co-operate with his old friends."

Another indication of encouraged "boosterism" supported by the ball club appeared in that same newsletter:

"HAVERHILL DRUGGIST PLANS 'MEET THE BRAVES' NIGHT"

"It is hard to point the finger at any one person in New England and call him or her the Braves' number one booster. However, a man who closely approximates that description is Arthur Peever, genial pharmacist from Haverhill. Peever is planning a 'Meet the Braves Night" in that town on June 5 and has worked with the diligence of a beaver to ascertain that things will go off letter perfect. Window displays featuring pictures of all Braves players, bats, balls and jackets have proclaimed to all that the 5th is to be a big day for the Braves in Haverhill. The new Tribal film, 'Take Me Out to the Wigwam' will be show, interesting speakers will round out the program. The entire proceeds are to be donated to a worthy charity. Good-natured Arthur Peever merits a great big hand from the good burghers of Haverhill for the time and effort he has expended in making the day a complete success."

57 Bob Brady, email to author, July 17, 2016.

58 Ken Coleman interview.

59 Regarding the BoSox Club, founded in 1967, Henry Berry said, "We've been around since 1964…so that makes them Johnnie-Come-Latelies." Brian Beaulieu, "Blohards Honor Bunts Berry, Then Watch Sox," *Boston Herald*, April 2, 1972: 49.

60 Henry T. Berry, "Happiness Is A Red Sox Victory," *New York Times*, September 2, 1979: CN20.

61 George Kimball, "The Maddening World of a BLOHARD in NY," *Boston Herald*, June 25, 1980: 31.

62 An article in the first BLOHARDS newsletter after Powers' death was headlined "'Leadership' Group Seen Comically Overmatched." Its first paragraph read: "Already staggered by the loss of James Powers, their "Beloved Helmsman," a beleaguered group of BLOHARD brass is now faced with the superhuman task of maintaining the administrative skills, grace and humor he brought to the organization. They are widely expected to fail."

63 John Cavanaugh, "Busy Days for Red Sox Fans," *New York Times*, July 3, 1983: CN14.

64 Thomas Rogers, "The Blohards Club," *New York Times*, June 23, 1980: C2. Amory wrote an article about the group, which appeared in Amory, "A Bronx Cheer for the Blohards," *Morning Star* (Rockford, Illinois), November 13, 1977: 11.

Joe Gergen, "Blohards Wait for Inevitable," *Newsday*, September 15, 1991: 2.

There is, as well, an anecdote often told by former *Boston Globe* writer and editor: "The Red Sox killed my father, and now they're coming after me." Among other places, this is re-told by David Halberstam, *The Teammates* (New York: Hyperion, 2003), 45.

[vii] Richard Bevilaqua, "Blohards: Sox Enclave in New York," *Boston Herald*, September 16, 1977: 30.number of newspapers. See, for instance, Cleveland Amory, "A Bronx Cheer for the Blohards," *Morning Star* (Rockford, Illinois), November 13, 1977: 11.

65 Joe Gergen, "Blohards Wait for Inevitable," *Newsday*, September 15, 1991: 2.

66 There is, as well, an anecdote often told by former *Boston Globe* writer and editor: "The Red Sox killed my father, and now they're coming after me." Among other places, this is re-told by David Halberstam, *The Teammates* (New York: Hyperion, 2003), 45.

67 Richard Bevilaqua, "Blohards: Sox Enclave in New York," *Boston Herald*, September 16, 1977: 30.

68 John Lacy, "The BLOHARDS Head for Fenway," *Hartford Courant*, April 4, 1979: 19.

69 Cavanagh.

70 Kevin Kernan, "It's A 'Hard' Life — Red Sox Fans in New York Might Supper More than Any," *New York Post*, June 27, 2004: 46.

71 "DiMaggio Head of Businessmen's BoSox Club," *Boston Herald*, February 16, 1967: 36.

72 Harold Kaese, "Dom Leads Off for BoSox Club."

73 Ibid.

74 "BOSOX New Sox Boosters Club," *Boston Record American*, February 16, 1967: 52. See also "DiMaggio to Head Hose Booster Club," *Boston Traveler*, February 16, 1967: 34. Both the Herald and the Record American published a photograph of 10 officers. Hanify was absent from the photograph.

75 Clif Keane, "Sox Open with Hope, High Praise," *Boston Globe*, April 11, 1967: 1.

76 Tim Horgan, "It's Logical To Tab Sox But Not Fair," *Boston Herald*, August 23, 1967: 49.

77 D. Leo Monahan, "Bruins Increase Price on Tickets," *Boston Record American*, August 13, 1967: 23,

78 Bill Liston, "Yaz Aids Jimmy On His 'Night'," *Boston Herald*, August 29, 1967: 37.

79 Russell Schneider, "Batting Around, *Cleveland Plain Dealer*, September 2, 1967: 32.

80 Garry Brown, "The Morning Line," *Springfield Union*, September 2, 1967: 44.

81 Fred Ciampa, "Sox Stars Give Awards," *Boston Record American*, September 30, 1967: 2.

82 Clif Keane, "Sox Rooters Florida Bound," *Boston Globe*, December 26, 1967: 22.

83 Will McDonough, "Cousy, Knicks Rumor Louder," *Boston Globe*, February 4, 1953: 53.

84 John Gillooly, "A.L. Champs to Have Sox Appeal on Road," *Boston Record American*, January 31, 1968: 14.

85 "BoSox Club Plans Royal Hose Welcome Hone," *Boston Record American*, February 17, 1968: 32.

86 "Teens Can Win Week at Ted Williams' Camp," *Boston Globe*, July 9, 1968: 23.

87 "Hawk Is Positive Thinker," *Boston Herald*, August 2, 1968: 34.

88 Bob Sales, "Sox Rip N.Y., Cling to 3rd," *Boston Globe*, September 28, 1968: 17.

89 United Press International, "Dom, Sox Club Ask Inter-league Play," *Boston Globe*, July 21, 1970: 24.

90 Dwight Chapin, "DiMaggios Back Together Again," *Los Angeles Times*, August 20, 1970: D11. The article quoted Dom as to the feeling behind the Club's resolution.

91 "28 Spring Sox Games," *Boston Herald*, November 15, 1970: 72.

92 Tim Horgan, "Sox Show Why Baseball Is Hurting," *Boston Herald*, February 4, 1971: 37.

93 A nice appreciation of host Anthony Athanas was provided by Nathan Cobb, "Peerless Anthony," *Boston Globe*, July 13, 1984: 18.

94 For more on Jackman, see The Cannonball Foundation at http://thecannonballfoundation.org/legend-cannonball-jackman/

95 Dick Dew, "Bosox Fan Club Most Successful in Major Leagues," *Boston Herald*, April 25, 1973: 34.

96 Kevin Mannix," Baseball Clinics A Big Hit," *Boston Herald*, July 19, 1974: 15.

97 See, for instance, a mention in the March 17, 1980 *Boston Herald*, under the headline "Another View of Winter Haven," on page 14.

98 Peter Gammons, "At 37, Yaz Still the Team's Most Valuable Player," *Boston Globe*, August 28, 1976: 22.

99 Kevin Mannix, "The BoSox Club Menu…It's Strictly Baseball," *Boston Herald*, April 23, 1978: 31.

100 "Sports," *Boston Herald*, May 10, 1978: 2.

101 Ernie Roberts, "The Devil and Mr. Allen," *Boston Globe*, December 20, 1975: 21.

102 Ernie Roberts, "Emerson Says Richards Can Help Nets," *Boston Globe*, June 4, 1977: 19.

103 Joe Fitzgerald, "Crowley Honored By BoSox Club," *Boston Herald*, November 21, 1981: 28.

104 Peter Gammons, "Red Sox Hold Off Yankees," *Boston Globe*, June 10, 1982: 1.

105 Carl Yastrzemski, "Yaz: The Final Days," *Boston Herald*, October 1, 1983: 47.

106 Leigh Montville, "One Last Fenway Go-Round for Yaz," *Boston Globe*, October 2, 1983: 1.

107 Garry Brown, "In Millers Falls, Those Red Sox Statistics Really Add Up," *Springfield Union*, June 9, 1985: 70.

108 Dan Shaughnessy, "Are Sox Out Of Position?" *Boston Globe*, June 29, 1986: 54.

109 Larry Whiteside, "Boyd Suspended By Red Sox," *Boston Globe*, July 12, 1986: 1.

110 Roger Clemens, with David Cataneo, "Clemens: I Was A Typical Fan," *Boston Herald*, May 18, 1987: 92.

111 Larry Whiteside, "Stanley Is Still Ailing," *Boston Globe*, July 3, 1987: 60.

112 Larry Whiteside, "HR, Injury for Evans," *Boston Globe*, September 19, 1988: 50.

113 Garry Brown, "Joe Morgan Becomes Oakland Athletics' Fan — For Now," *Springfield Union-News*, October 1, 1988: 6.

114 Dan Shaughnessy, "Sox Camp Still Abuzz," *Boston Globe*, March 20, 1989: 35.

115 Pumpsie Green's story and the overall context is examined at length in Bill Nowlin, ed., *Pumpsie and Progress: The Red Sox, Race, and Redemption* (Burlington, Massachusetts: Rounder Books, 2010.)

116 Steve Fainaru, "In Racism's Shadow Red Sox Working to Shed Longtime Image, but Blacks In and Out of Baseball Still Uneasy," *Boston Globe*, August 4, 1991.

117 Bill Nowlin, *Mr. Red Sox: The Johnny Pesky Story* (Cambridge, Massachusetts: Rounder Books, 2012), 308-9.

118 Beth Carney and Jim Sullivan, "Party with the Pasha," *Boston Globe*, May 4, 2000: E2.

119 Beth Carney and Jim Sullivan, "Newton Group Curbs Violence with Music," *Boston Globe*, May 26, 2000: D2.

120 Christina Pazzanese, "Diehard Fans Seek A Sequel — to 1918," *Boston Globe* (West edition), August 12, 2004: 1.

121 David Laurila, "Originally from Dot, Always at Fenway; 17 Rows Above the Red Sox Bullpen, A Close Observer," *Boston Globe*, October 17, 2004: 6.

122 See a tribute to him: Bella English, "In the End, A Happy Red Sox Fan," *Boston Globe*, August 21, 2005: 9.

123 Bill Nowlin, *Fenway Lives* (Burlington, Massachusetts: Rounder Books, 2004), 114, 117.

124 It's not fully clear what was meant by "of its kind" because Ken Coleman and several of the other founders knew that at least the Wahoo Club was an older booster club.

125 Email from Paul Boghosian, January 3, 2017.

126 Marvin Pave, "Dick Bresciani, Red Sox VP of Public Affairs, At 76," *Boston Globe*, December 5, 2014: B8.

127 Stan Grossfeld, "Kennedys Always Faithful to Red Sox," *Boston Globe*, July 20, 2016: D1.